OCR
Medieval History
RAIDERS AND INVADERS
POWER AND CONTROL

COLIN SHEPHARD

ROSEMARY REES

HODDER
EDUCATION
AN HACHETTE UK COMPANY

Orders: please contact Bookpoint Ltd, 130 Milton Park, Abingdon, Oxon OX14 4SB. Telephone: +44 (0)1235 827720. Fax: +44 (0)1235 400454. Lines are open from 9.00a.m. to 6.00p.m., Monday to Saturday, with a 24-hour message answering service. Visit our website at www.hoddereducation.co.uk

First published in 2007
by Hodder Education,
an Hachette UK company
338 Euston Road
London NW1 3BH

Impression number   4 3
Year   2010 2009

Layouts by Black Dog Design
Artwork by Jon Davis/Linden Artists, Richard Duszczak, Tony Jones/Art Construction
Typeset in 11pt Bodoni Book by Black Dog Design
Printed in Italy

A catalogue record for this title is available from the British Library

ISBN-10: 0 340 92738 0
ISBN-13: 978 0 340 92738 0

Contents

Acknowledgements

Photo credits

Cover *l* By permission of the British Library (MS Add. 22493 f.1), *r* Courtesy of The Knights of Royal England www.knightsroyal.co.uk; **p.4** Alan Sorrell; **p.7** *l* The British Museum, London/The Bridgeman Art Library, *c* TopFoto/The British Museum/HIP, *r* National Trust/Fisheye Images www.nationaltrust.org.uk; **p.8** © English Heritage Photo Library; **p.9** British Library, London/The Bridgeman Art Library; **p.10** *t* © Norwich Castle Museum and Art Gallery, *bl* Andrew Palmer/ Alamy, *br* © English Heritage (drawn by Karen Guffogg); **p.11** *t* © Norwich Castle Museum and Art Gallery, *b* TopFoto/British Library/HIP; **p.13** © English Heritage Photo Library; **p.15** *l & r* © The Trustees of The British Museum.; **p.16** *l* © English Heritage Photo Library, *r* © B. Norman/Ancient Art & Architecture Collection; **p.17** *l* Reproduced courtesy of the Order of the Holy Paraclete, St. Hilda's Priory, *r* British Library, London/The Bridgeman Art Library; **p.19** *l* © Antony Wootten, *r* Viking Ship Museum, Oslo, Norway/The Bridgeman Art Library; **p.22** *tl* © Ashmolean Museum, University of Oxford/The Bridgeman Art Library, *tr* The British Museum, London/The Bridgeman Art Library, *b* © Museum of London/The Bridgeman Art Library; **p.23** *Alfred the Saxon King in the Tent of Guthrum the Dane* by Daniel Maclise, Laing Art Gallery (Tyne and Wear Museums); **p.24** The British Museum, London/The Bridgeman Art Library; **p.25** Courtesy Murton Park; **p.26** © R. Sheridan/ Ancient Art & Architecture Collection; **p.27** *l* Werner Forman Archive/by Courtesy of the Royal Commission on Historical Monuments, *r* © York Archaeological Trust; **p.28** © Victor Ambrus; **p.29** © York Archaeological Trust; **p.32** *tl & c* akg-images/Erich Lessing, *tr & b* TopFoto/Woodmansterne; **p.33** *l & r* TopFoto/Woodmansterne; **p.35** © Dick Clark/Mayhem Photographics; **p.37** *t* Mary Evans Picture Library, *b* © English Heritage Photo Library; **p.40** British Library, London/The Bridgeman Art Library; **p.41** © English Heritage (painted by Ivan Lapper); **p.44** © C.M. Dixon/Ancient Art & Architecture Collection; **p.45** *t* © Norwich Castle Museum and Art Gallery, *b* TopFoto/The British Museum/HIP; **p.46** akg-images/Erich Lessing; **p.62** British Library, London/The Bridgeman Art Library; **p.63** Reproduced by permission of the Provost and Fellows of Eton College; **p.65** National Portrait Gallery, London/ The Bridgeman Art Library; **p.68** Walt Disney Pictures/The Kobal Collection; **p.69** R H Productions/Robert Harding; p.70 *l & r* Icon/Ladd Co/Paramount/The Kobal Collection; **p.71** TopFoto; **p.79** *t* Royal Exchange, London/The Bridgeman Art Library, *b* Houses of Parliament, Westminster, London/The Bridgeman Art Library; **p.84** Mary Evans Picture Library; **p.87** Malcolm Fife/Alamy; **p.100** Private Collection/The Stapleton Collection/The Bridgeman Art Library; **p.105** Mary Evans Picture Library; **p.109** *tl* © Rob Watkins, *tr* © B. Crisp/Ancient Art & Architecture Collection, *b* With Agnew's; **p.110** *tl* TopFoto/British Library/HIP, *tc* Mary Evans Picture Library, *tr* Mary Evans/Bill Meadows, *bl* Walt Disney Pictures/The Kobal Collection; **p.111** *tl* Mary Evans Picture Library, *tc* By permission of the British Library (MS Cotton Julius E. IV f.6), *tr* TopFoto/HIP, *bl* National Portrait Gallery, London (NPG D18890), *br* Icon/Ladd Co/Paramount/The Kobal Collection; **p.112** *tl* akg-images/VISIOARS, *tc* National Portrait Gallery, London/The Bridgeman Art Library, *tr & bl* Mary Evans Picture Library, *br* TopFoto.

Written sources

p.43 *S4* John Blair *The Anglo-Saxon Age* OUP, 2000, by permission of Oxford University Press; **p.44** *S8* Julian Richards *The Blood of the Vikings* Hodder and Stoughton, 1996; **p.46** *S12* extract from Rudyard Kipling 'Danegeld', published in *Rudyard Kipling: The Complete Verse* Kyle Cathie, 1990, by permission of A P Watt Ltd on behalf of The National Trust for Places of Historic Interest or Natural Beauty; **p.47** *S19* John Blair *The Anglo-Saxon Age* OUP, 2000, by permission of Oxford University Press; **p.68** *SD Newnes Pictorial Knowledge*; **p.72** *S1* Austin Lane Poole *From Domesday Book to Magna Carta 1087–1216* OUP, 1951; **p.93** *S1* www.bbc.co.uk/history; **p.104** *S1 & 2* www.100welshheroes.com, *S3* Gwyn A Williams *When Was Wales* Penguin, 1985; **p.113** *S2* Austin Lane Poole *From Domesday Book to Magna Carta 1087–1216* OUP, 1951; **p.114** *S8* Simon Schama *A History of Britain: At the Edge of the World? 3000BC–AD1603* BBC Worldwide, 2000, *S11* www.britannica.com; **p.115** *S12* The Online Reference Book for Medieval Studies http://the-orb.net, *S13* Norman Davies *The Isles: A History* Macmillan, 1999; **p.115** *S17* www.bbc.co.uk/history, *S18* Simon Schama *A History of Britain: At the Edge of the World? 3000BC–AD1603* BBC Worldwide, 2000, *S20* Glanmor Williams *Owen Glendower* OUP, 1966; **p.117** *S21* www.castlewales.com/home, *S22* quoted in Chris Barber *In Search of Owain Glyndwr* Blorenge Books, 1998, *S23* www.100welshheroes.com, *S24* Oxford Dictionary of National Biography OUP, 2004.

Every effort has been made to trace all copyright holders but, if any have been inadvertently overlooked, the Publishers will be pleased to make the necessary arrangements at the first opportunity.

t = top, *b* = bottom, *l* = left, *r* = right, *c* = centre

Part 1 Raiders and invaders

How to use the material in Part 1

This part of the book covers Module 1 of the Specification and is about the Saxons, Vikings and Normans – the people who raided, invaded and settled in the British Isles between around 400 and 1100.

You will be using a wide range of sources to investigate why raids and invasions happened, and how the Saxons, Vikings and Normans settled. Indeed, it is through the use of sources that you will build up a picture of these people. The three chapters – Saxons, Vikings and Normans – also give you enough basic information to enable you to put into context the sources you are dealing with and the inferences and conclusions you have drawn from them.

Although the approach in the book is broadly chronological, you will be expected, as you work through each chapter, to compare and contrast what happened, and the different ways in which we know, or think we know, about what happened.

Think particularly about:

- What were the reasons for the invasions?
- How were the invasions organised and why were they successful?
- How did the invaders settle?
- How effectively did the invaders establish control?
- What were the long-term legacies of the invasions?
- How do we find out about the invasions?
- How have these invasions been represented and interpreted?

There are questions and tasks as you work through each chapter, and summary tasks at the end, which expect you to reflect on what you have learned and compare and contrast what you have found out with what you learned from an earlier chapter.

After the three main chapters, you will find a 'ragbag' of sources. This contains a range of different sources on Saxons, Vikings and Normans for you to dip into as you work through the different chapters, to use when answering the summary questions and to refer to when you do the externally set exam question. Sometimes, it will be suggested that you look in the ragbag, but mostly it's up to you.

An important part of your learning is the research that you do. Sometimes you will find yourself directed to a specific internet site, and in Chapter 1.3 The Normans there is a structured piece of research for you to undertake. Certainly in the externally set task you will be expected to follow through a research task, and an example of how to work through one of these is given to you after the ragbag.

It is essential, therefore, that you use this book as a starting point for your investigations – not as the finishing line!

Timeline of Saxon, Viking and Norman raiding, invading and settling

This timeline shows you the sequence of raiding, invading and settling events. Refer to it whenever you have a concern about where something fits in.

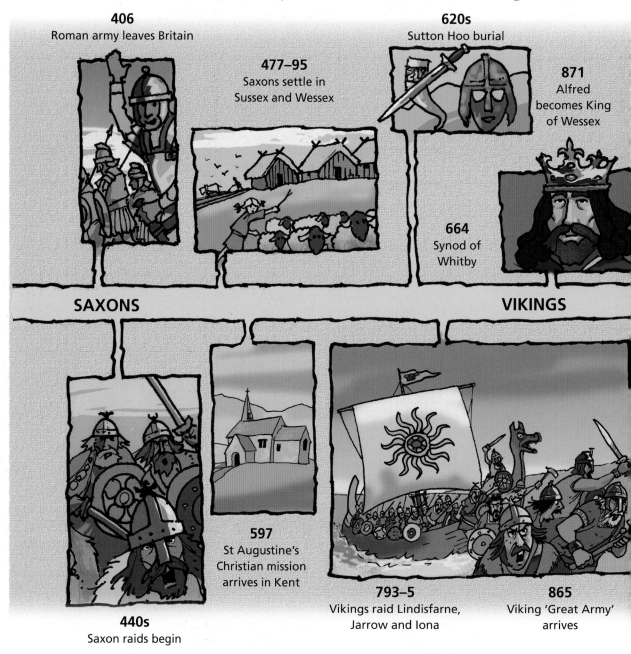

406
Roman army leaves Britain

477–95
Saxons settle in
Sussex and Wessex

620s
Sutton Hoo burial

871
Alfred
becomes King
of Wessex

664
Synod of
Whitby

SAXONS

VIKINGS

597
St Augustine's
Christian mission
arrives in Kent

793–5
Vikings raid Lindisfarne,
Jarrow and Iona

865
Viking 'Great Army'
arrives

440s
Saxon raids begin

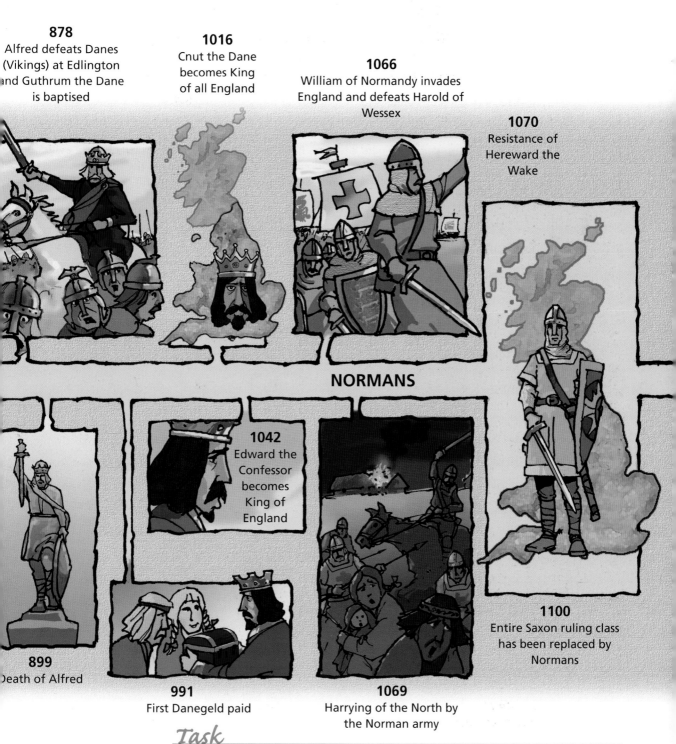

878
Alfred defeats Danes (Vikings) at Edlington and Guthrum the Dane is baptised

1016
Cnut the Dane becomes King of all England

1066
William of Normandy invades England and defeats Harold of Wessex

1070
Resistance of Hereward the Wake

NORMANS

1042
Edward the Confessor becomes King of England

899
Death of Alfred

991
First Danegeld paid

1069
Harrying of the North by the Norman army

1100
Entire Saxon ruling class has been replaced by Normans

Task

Copy the dates on this timeline into your file but leave large gaps in between each date. As you work through this section and do your own research, add events, dates and people in the correct places. In this way you will gradually build up a detailed chronology of the period.

The Saxons

Britain had, by AD 380, been part of the Roman Empire for over three hundred years. A snapshot of the Roman province of Britain at this time would find Roman soldiers patrolling Hadrian's Wall, the northernmost boundary of the Empire; the Wall, together with strong eastern coastal defences, would be keeping enemies of the Empire at bay. South of the Wall, the whole of the country was under Roman rule – a province that was just one small part of the vast and powerful empire that dominated the Mediterranean and most of Western Europe. Fifty years later this had ended for the British. Archaeological evidence points to a sudden and total collapse of the Roman way of life in Britain between, roughly, 411 and 430. At the beginning of the fifth century AD the Roman Empire was attacked by tribes massing on its borders: Franks, Vandals, Huns, Ostrogoths and Visigoths, who all wanted a share in the Empire's wealth and, more importantly, its land. In AD 410 and again in AD 455, these 'barbarians', as the Romans called them, captured Rome itself. The Roman Empire was collapsing. What, in Britain, would take its place?

Raiding, then invading

● SOURCE 1

Alan Sorrell's reconstruction of a Saxon raiding party landing in open boats on the Yorkshire coast near Scarborough.

What is happening here? In the background, Roman signal towers send the alarm to the nearest military garrison. This is a picture drawn from the artist's imagination but it is based on fact. We know the Saxons raided the east coast while the Romans still occupied Britain; we know that the Romans set up an elaborate system of warning beacons in the event of just such an action; and we know that the Saxons crossed the North Sea in great open rowing boats. The artist put all this together, being as true to the past as possible.

Why did the Saxons invade Britain?

We can get other clues about the early Saxons from a British monk called Gildas. As you will see, he was hardly a fan of the Saxons! The title of his work gives you a clue, even before you read what he says:

● SOURCE 2

All the councillors, together with that proud tyrant Gurthrigern, the British king, were so blinded that they sealed their country's doom by inviting in among them [like wolves into the sheepfold] the fierce and impious Saxons, a race hateful to both God and man, to repel the invasions of the northern nations. They first landed on the eastern side of the island, and there fixed their sharp talons, apparently to fight in favour of the island but alas! more truly against it. Their motherland, finding her first brood thus successful, sends forth a larger company of her wolfish offspring, which, sailing over, join themselves to their bastard-born comrades.

Gildas wrote *The Ruin of Britain* around the 540s. The 'proud tyrant Gurthrigern' is probably Vortigern.

The Venerable Bede, another monk writing later on, tells us where these raiders and invaders came from:

● SOURCE 3

They came from three very powerful Germanic tribes, the Saxons, Angles and Jutes. From the Saxon country, that is, the district now known as Old Saxony, came the East Saxons, the South Saxons and the West Saxons. [He goes on:] It was not long before such hordes of these alien peoples crowded into the island that the natives who had invited them began to live in terror. These heathen conquerors devastated the surrounding cities and countryside and established a stranglehold over nearly all the doomed island.

Bede wrote his *Ecclesiastical History of the English People* in 731.

- Sources 1–3 tell you quite a lot about the Saxons, but they all have their problems. What are they?
- Do these sources give you any firm clues about why the Saxons came to Britain?

Further clues about why the Saxons came to Britain can be seen in the findings of archaeologists working at Feddersen Wierde, near the mouth of the River Weiser on the European side of the North Sea. They discovered the remains of large wooden buildings that were abandoned around 450 because of rising sea levels. Add to this the invitation from Vortigern to come across and work as mercenaries and the rich fertile lowlands of southern and eastern Britain, and we probably have all the main reasons why the Saxons left their homelands. Remember, too, that Saxons had been raiding the east coast of Britain for over 200 years. They would have a pretty good idea of the rich pickings to be had there.

There are very few sources of evidence about the fifth and sixth centuries. There is some archaeological evidence, mainly objects from graves, but only fragmentary evidence from the Saxons themselves about the ways in which they lived out their lives once they arrived in Britain. So, much of what we know about their early years in Britain comes from angry, outraged British monks, from foreigners who were not directly involved and from half-remembered Saxon stories and traditions that surfaced later. It is not until the 600s that we can begin to be certain about what was going on in Saxon England.

How did the Saxons establish themselves in Britain?

Britain was not an empty island when the Saxons arrived in force in the 440s. True, most of the Romans had gone, and Saxon raiding parties must have told people in their homelands of this. The Roman army had left in 406; four years later the Roman Emperor had ordered the cities of Britain to look after their own defences. Who remained? Some part-Roman, part-British families who had nowhere else to go and, of course, the Britons themselves, some of whom had lived on the fringe of the Roman Empire and had maybe never seen a Roman in their lives. What were these people to do, faced with a collapsed economy, disintegrating society and the withdrawal of support? Were they going to be easy prey for raiders and invaders from across the North Sea?

One of the things they could do, of course, was to ask for help. In 446 the Britons appealed to Aetius, the last effective Roman governor in Gaul. They asked him to hear 'for the third time [the] groans of the Britons'. They told him that 'the barbarians drive us to the sea; the sea throws us back on the barbarians. Thus two modes of death await us, we are either slain or drowned.' The other thing they could do was to fight back. And they did that, too. Have a look in the ragbag (page 43) and see what Nennius has to say.

The Venerable Bede tells us that 449 was the year of the *Adventus Saxonum*, the coming of the Saxons. It is more than probable that the Saxons, Hengist and Horsa, invited in by Vortigern to act as mercenaries in his defence of Britain, eventually turned against him (look back to page 5 at what Gildas says) and set up their own kingdom in Kent. Wave after wave of Saxon invasions followed. For example, Aelle, in 477, began setting up the Saxon kingdom of Sussex and Cerdic and Cynric, in 495, founded the kingdom of Wessex. British resistance was easily overcome initially, although the Saxon advance was slowed down by the British victory at Mount Badon, where they were fighting under the leadership of Ambrosius Aurelianus. Around 550, the Saxons were on the move again, pushing the British further and further west and north. By 610, after the Battle of Chester, the Saxons were in control of most of what we now call England.

Task

Historians are generally agreed that the following dates and battles are reasonably accurate in showing the spread of Saxons throughout Britain.

455 Aegelsthrep	456 Crecganford	491 Andredesceaster
500 Badon	552 Searoburh	556 Beranburh
571 Bedcanford	577 Deorham	610 Chester

1 **Find out** who was involved in each battle. Try typing them into a search engine like Google, or use a good reference book in your library.

2 **Work out** how each was significant in the Saxon advance.

3 **Decide** how best to present this information, remembering you have to deal with three elements: time, place and significance.

4 **And then do it!**

How well did the Saxons settle the country?

The first Saxons were rural people. There is very little evidence that they took over the abandoned Roman towns, some of which, of course, had been abandoned for the second time by the Romano-British as the invading Saxons pushed them further west and north. It seems that most early Saxons probably looked on the crumbling Roman towns and paved roads with awe, seeing them as the 'cunning work of giants' and not as the work of human beings. Even so, the Saxons had a word for town, *ceaster*, and often showed that they knew its Roman name. The Roman *Mamucion* became the Saxon *Mameceaster* (modern Manchester), for example. And it must have been tempting, many cities having walls and most being at road junctions, for war lords to use them temporarily as good defensible positions when they were desperately trying to hold on to the land they had won.

Kings and kingdoms

The 600s saw the gradual coming together of groups of invaders to form larger kingdoms – roughly a dozen by the end of the century. The process wasn't simple: small kingdoms emerged and vanished without much trace, larger kingdoms fought to extend their power base or absorbed others when a ruler died and there was no clear internal support for a successor.

- Read what Bede says about King Oswine of Deira. What sort of problems would a society have that contained a number of kingdoms like this one?

● **SOURCE 4**

King Oswine was tall and handsome, pleasant of speech, courteous in manner, and generous to nobles and commons alike; so it came about that noblemen from almost every kingdom flocked to serve him as retainers.

The Venerable Bede, seventh century.

In the early Saxon years, a king's followers or 'thegns' were more tied to their king than they were to their land. They were expected to live with him in his great hall, follow him, work for him, fight for him and, if necessary, die for him. Look in the ragbag (page 43) and you'll find a source by Bede. It's part of a story he is telling about King Eadwine but, without doing so deliberately, Bede also paints a marvellous picture of life in a great hall. Unwitting testimony like this is sometimes the best evidence of all. Why?

Sutton Hoo: a king's ship burial

The evidence we can gather from the ship burial of Sutton Hoo near Woodbridge in Suffolk is of a quite different sort. It seems to date from the 620s and is probably (although historians and archaeologists are still arguing about it) the burial place of King Raedwald, King of the East Anglians.

● **SOURCE 5**

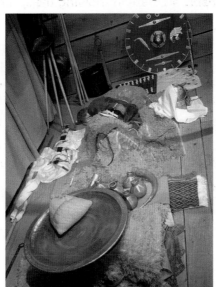

Some of the objects found in the Sutton Hoo burial. The picture on the right shows a reconstruction of the burial.

Here is some information about the objects found in the Sutton Hoo burial, some of which you can see in Source 5:

1 The helmet is typically late Roman but the bronze work on it is similar to that found in east Sweden.
2 The great buckle is a complicated design of animals, snakes and bird heads made from gold and a mixture of sulphur and silver. It is hollow with a hinged back. This needed complicated techniques and technology to make.
3 Two silver spoons, one of which had the Greek word *Paulos* inscribed on it and the other, *Saulos*.
4 A great silver dish from Byzantium that was made between 491 and 518.
5 Among the other treasures from the tomb were coins from Gaul.

What does this archaeological evidence tell us about the early Saxons in general, and this king in particular? (Hint: think about time and space, communications, technology and wealth.)

Ad Gefrin: a king's palace

Source 6 is a reconstruction of Ad Gefrin, a royal settlement in Northumberland. It is based on archaeological evidence, and shows how it may have looked in about 627 during a visit by King Edwin. Soon afterwards, arsonists struck, and the royal palace burned to the ground.

- Do you think there were any differences between the lifestyles of the occupier of the Sutton Hoo ship burial and Ad Gefrin? Explain your answer.
- Look in the ragbag (page 44) and you'll find an internet site about Yeavering, another name for Ad Gefrin. Write a paragraph explaining whether or not you would recommend this site to a friend who wanted to find out about Ad Gefrin.

● **SOURCE 6**

Peter Dunn's reconstruction of Ad Gefrin.

The importance of land

By the tenth century, many thegns had a great deal of power and influence. In return for services to their king, they were rewarded with weapons, horses, valuable gifts and the 'joys of the hall', as Bede described. But the most valuable gift was the gift of land. It was land that kept the thegns loyal to their king; land that meant Saxons could settle in communities under the direction of the thegns, and land that could bring prosperity. Land meant power.

Managing the kingdoms: Witans

Saxon kings had to manage their lands and from time to time they called their thegns together in a Witan – an assembly of 'wise men'. To their thegns some kings would add bishops and abbots of monasteries. Witans would not always meet in the same place and would not always consist of the same people. It all depended on who the king was and where he was on his royal estates. Usually a Witan could only offer advice when asked, and even then the king could make up his own mind what to do.

But at least his decisions had been heard by the most powerful people in his lands and stood a good chance of being implemented. As kingdoms grew larger and meetings of the Witan became more important, some members were given specialised work – responsibility for trade, or coinage, for example.

- Look at this Saxon painting of a Witan. Can you work out what is happening here? What does it tell us about Witans?

● **SOURCE 7**

A Saxon Witan.

The ordinary people

Evidence about the ways in which ordinary people lived their lives is difficult to find. The early chroniclers were monks, keen to record the deeds of saints and holy people as well as the kings, good, bad and indifferent. Even then, as you have seen, this evidence is limited. It is even more limited when we ask about ordinary Saxon men, women and children. Nevertheless, it has been possible for historians, working on, for example, documents containing early laws, and working with archaeologists, to piece together a picture of what life for Saxon people was like.

It must be remembered, however, that the Saxon period covered about 600 years. During this time there were many changes. For example, the population increased; more land was brought under cultivation; towns and ports grew; trade developed and government became more complicated in order to deal with a more complex society. Change didn't happen all at once, nor did it happen in the same way in different places. When you research Saxon England, be careful to check out the date and the place of your findings.

It is possible, however, to tease out certain characteristics that were common to the everyday lives of most Saxons and that make it possible for us to identify them as Saxon, and not Norman or Viking or British.

Ceorls and thralls

The Saxons were rural people. Most ordinary people in the kingdoms were free-men, called *ceorls*, although there were slaves, too, generally called *thralls*. Many thralls were descended from the original British people who inhabited the British Isles before the Saxons invaded; some were prisoners taken in battles between the kingdoms; and others were criminals who couldn't pay their fines. In hard times, Saxon parents could sell their children into slavery: there would be fewer mouths to feed and money to buy much needed food. The children of thralls automatically became thralls themselves, and so slavery continued throughout Saxon times, even though it was officially disapproved of by the Church.

● **SOURCE 8**

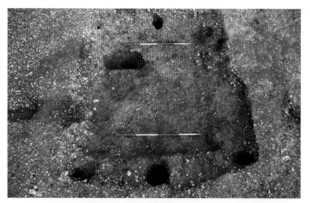

The postholes, showing where a Saxon hut once stood, were uncovered by archaeologists in Norfolk.

Where did ordinary people live?

There are no drawings, paintings or carvings from these early Saxon times to tell us what the homes of ordinary people looked like, and very little by way of written descriptions. Historians skilled at reconstruction have had to rely heavily on archaeological evidence. Most Saxon houses, barns and great halls were built from wood that has long since rotted away, but chemical analysis of the staining in the surrounding earth and the unearthing of postholes has enabled reconstructions to be built.

• What conclusions can you draw from the differences between the two reconstructions in Sources 9 and 10?

● **SOURCE 9**

A physical reconstruction of an early Saxon hut, built at the Weald and Downland Museum, Singleton, Sussex. This was probably the most typical type of peasant building between the fifth and eighth centuries.

● **SOURCE 10**

Karen Guffogg's reconstruction of eleventh-century Saxon houses in Norwich, Norfolk.

Working people

As Saxon society grew settled and more complex, Saxons became specialised in the work they did. They worked, for example, as bakers and shoemakers, goldsmiths and ship builders, merchants and sailors. But the first Saxon invaders worked the land. They had to: they needed to survive. Throughout the whole Saxon period, most people worked in agriculture.

Villages and farming

The first Saxons took over land worked by the Britons, but gradually they began to clear forest and plough moorland. Small, scattered homesteads developed into village communities that were more or less self-sufficient. Each ceorl worked at least one hide of land. This was the amount of land reckoned to be sufficient to support a family. The actual size of a hide seems to have been somewhere between fifty and a hundred acres. By 1066, most Saxons were farming parcels

● **SOURCE 11**

A photograph of the iron cutting blade from a Saxon plough.

of land in great open fields. Cereals were the main crops grown – barley, rye and wheat – along with peas, beans and flax. These, along with bees to produce honey for sweetening – sustained most villages at a basic level. Barley was used to brew beer; rye and wheat in bread making and flax was spun and woven into a coarse cloth. Sheep and cows, pigs and hens would provide milk and eggs, meat and wool.

- • What conclusions can you draw from Sources 11 and 12 about agriculture in Saxon times?

● **SOURCE 12**

Saxons ploughing: a drawing made in about 900.

Most Saxon villages had a lord – usually one of the king's thegns – to whom villagers looked for protection. A thegn would have several villages for which he was responsible. He had a good share of the land, which the ceorls and thralls worked for him. In exchange for his protection, the villagers not only worked the thegn's land but they paid him 'food rent' in pigs, eggs, milk or whatever it was they produced.

Not everyone in Saxon villages was directly involved in farming. Some, for example, were blacksmiths, making and mending ploughs and scythes, pots and pans. Most Saxon homes did their own baking and brewing – usually the responsibility of the women.

Task

Archaeologists and historians have tried to reconstruct Saxon villages. One has been built at West Stow in Suffolk on the site of an original Saxon village. Go to www.stedmundsbury.gov.uk and follow the links from there. How far does this reconstruction help your understanding of what a Saxon village would have been like?

Could ceorls become thegns?

It seems that they could. This means that Saxon society was pretty fluid and that an upwardly mobile ceorl could become a person of power and influence. This is what Archbishop Wulfstan had to say:

● SOURCE 13

If a ceorl prospered so that he possessed fully five hides of land of his own, a church and a kitchen, a bell and a fortress-gate, a seat and a special office in the king's hall, he was worthy thereafter to be called a thegn.

Archbishop Wulfstan, writing in about 1000.

How did towns develop?

Archaeologists are providing more and more evidence about the ways in which towns developed. One of these towns was Hamwic, which is now the modern Southampton.

Task

1 Use the internet to look up Hamwic. Just type Hamwic into your search engine and see what happens. Use the information you find to explain how and why the town developed.

2 Now go to www.portcities.org.uk/london and find out what archaeologists think Saxon London was like.

3 Which of the sites you have visited (and you don't have to limit yourself to the ones you looked at in questions 1 and 2) have you found the most useful in helping you understand how towns developed?

Could the Saxons get justice?

Family loyalties were basic to the Saxon system of justice. Safety, for that is what justice is supposed to bring, lay in the certain knowledge that relatives would avenge one's death. To make this possible, everyone had a life-price – a *wergild*. Thegns, obviously, were worth more than ceorls who, in their turn, were worth more than thralls. In early Wessex a thegn's wergild was six times that of a ceorl. So if, for example, a Saxon was murdered, the murderer had to pay the appropriate wergild in full to the victim's family and honour would be satisfied. Kings and church leaders encouraged the peaceful payment of dues, in money or in goods. But if the wrongdoer could not, or would not, pay, then the victim's family was entitled to pursue a blood feud. Some crimes, such as treachery to one's lord, were so awful that compensation was not enough. Only death was sufficient repayment.

Saxon law recognised that there could be a clash between loyalty to one's family and loyalty to one's lord. King Alfred's laws allowed any man 'to fight on behalf of his born kinsman, if he is being wrongfully attacked, except against his lord, for that we do not allow.'

Saxons held regular open-air meetings called folk moots, which dealt with law-breakers. The accused person swore a solemn oath that he was innocent and produced oath-helpers who would swear that the oath was true. The value of an oath-helper depended on his rank, where the word of a thegn counted for more than that of a thrall. If enough oath-helpers of the right sort swore a person was innocent, then they were. If not enough oath-helpers could be found, guilt or innocence was determined by ordeal. The accused was given the choice of iron or water. The choice of water meant that the accused was thrown into a pond or river. If innocent, the person would sink; if guilty, the person would float to the surface. The thinking here was that the water would cast out the guilty yet receive the innocent. The choice of iron meant that the accused had to grasp a red hot iron bar. If, when the bandages were removed three days later, the burn had healed, then the person was innocent. The thinking here was that God would help the innocent. Where a woman was accused of a crime, her brother, husband or father would stand in for her.

Discussion point

Can you find any similarities between the Saxon system of justice and the system of justice operating in Britain today? (Hint: what importance is still put on oath making in British courts today?)

Case study: Were the Saxons Christians?

● SOURCE 14

A drawing of a Saxon nobleman's residence at Porchester. Can you see a square stone tower in roughly the middle of his estate? This may have been part of a private church.

- Look at this reconstruction (Source 14). It was put together as a result of excavations on the Roman fortress at Porchester in Hampshire, which was built in the 200s to repel Saxon invaders. This is what reconstruction experts thought the site looked like in the 900s. What has happened here?
- Can you guess at the significance of having a church made from stone and dwellings made from wood and thatch?
- And a church in the middle of your private dwellings?
- Does this mean that all Saxons were Christians?

You can make reasonable guesses at answers to all these questions, but you'll need to search out other sources of evidence, including what historians say happened, to see whether or not your guesses are on the right tracks.

The pagan Saxons

We have seen that monks (Gildas, Nennius and Bede) wrote the history of early Saxon times. So quite obviously, Christianity was established in Britain before the Saxons arrived. Equally obviously, the Christian monks were not going to write favourably about people they regarded not only as raiders and invaders, but pagans as well. You will be able to find examples of the terrible things these monks said about the pagan Saxons. The Saxons brought with them their own beliefs and their own gods. Their principle gods were Tiw, Woden and Thor. These names are still part of our language in Tuesday, Wednesday and Thursday and in some place-names, like Wednesbury in Staffordshire and Thursley in Surrey. Even after they converted to Christianity (see below), the Saxons named a religious festival after one of their old pagan gods. Saxons made shrines to their gods in remote places and some of their names are still in our language, too: Peper Harow in Surrey and Harrow-on-the-Hill in what was once Middlesex, for example, are named after the Saxon word *hearg* that means 'shrine'. The Christian Church was later to forbid the worship of 'stones, wood, trees and wells' so we must assume that the Saxons venerated these. Steadily, though, the Christian British were pushed west and north, into parts of the country that remained free from pagan invasion.

The conversion of the Saxons to Christianity

In 597 the Roman Catholic Church was so worried about the position of the Christian Church in Britain that Pope Gregory launched a mission to convert the pagan English (Saxon) parts of the country. The Roman monk Augustine, who headed up the mission, was advised to work with the power structure within Saxon society, and so he started by converting the rulers. This top-down conversion worked well, and by the end of the 600s, all the English kings and their courts had converted to Christianity. This meant that, in name at least, their people had too. It also meant that from the outset, English (Saxon) Christianity was firmly associated with political power. Wherever possible, old Roman buildings were adopted as Christian churches, especially when it was believed they had been churches when Britain was part of the Roman Empire. In this way the Roman Catholic Church emphasised its links with the past not only by using existing churches but also by continuing to recognise the authority of Rome and the Pope.

But Saxon conversion to Christianity wasn't quite as neat and tidy as it sounds.

Task

1 Look back to the grave goods of the East Anglian ruler King Raedwald, who died in about 620. Are there any clues here as to whether he had converted to Christianity or not?

2 Find out what other grave goods were in the ship burial and so confirm what you suspect.

Bede, however, says this about Raedwald:

● SOURCE 15

Raedwald had long before received Christian baptism in Kent, but to no good purpose. On his return home, his wife and certain perverse advisers persuaded him to apostatise from the true Faith. He tried to serve both Christ and the ancient gods, and he had in the same temple an altar for the holy sacrifice of Christ side by side with an altar on which victims were offered to devils.

Bede, writing about Raedwald's conversion to Christianity.

• What conclusion can you now draw about King Raedwald's religious beliefs?

Look now at the gilt buckles excavated from a Saxon grave in Faversham, Kent and at the gold necklet excavated from a Saxon cemetery at Desborough in Northamptonshire.

● SOURCE 16

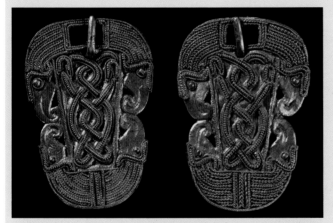

These miniature buckles were found amongst burials in King's Field, Faversham, Kent and date from the early seventh century AD. They are decorated with two pairs of bird's heads. Archaeologists believe that the combination of two birds refers to the Viking god Odin who, according to legend, was accompanied by two ravens.

● SOURCE 17

This gold and garnet necklet has a central cross, indicating that the woman who wore it was a convert to Christianity.

• Look back to what you decided about King Raedwald's religious beliefs. What can you now say about the spread of Christianity throughout Saxon England?

We know that in 627 King Eadwine of Northumbria welcomed the Roman missionary Paulinus to his court and was baptised along with all his thegns. But on Eadwine's defeat and death five years later, Paulinus had to flee the court as everyone reverted to their old religion. It seems that, while Roman Christianity could take a hold amongst the ruling Saxons, it took much longer for ordinary people to be convinced.

This is a reconstruction of the inside of an early timber Christian church at Lindisfarne, as it might have been in 650. The church, of which nothing now remains, would probably have been built of oak and thatch, like Irish churches of the time.

Celtic Christianity

In the Celtic west, however, matters had taken a different turn. Christianity here was less concerned with rulers and with power and far more concerned with establishing grass-roots contact with ordinary people. Here Christianity flourished in small, locally based monasteries, which by the year 600 had contacts with Scotland, Gaul and Italy. When the Christian King Oswald won control of Northumbria, he turned to the Irish monks in the Scottish monastery of Iona (off the coast of Mull) for a missionary to come over and convert his people. The monk Aidan came across and helped establish a Celtic religious community on Lindisfarne, off the Northumbrian coast.

● **SOURCE 19**

This photograph is of a tiny (7m x 4m) Saxon church at Escomb, Co. Durham, which was almost certainly built in the seventh or eighth century.

- Is it possible that two such different churches could have been built at roughly the same time and in the same area? Must one of the images be wrong?
- If both images are correct, what conclusions can you draw about the Christian Church at this time?

Celtic and Roman Christianity collide: the Synod of Whitby in 664

It was almost inevitable that the two sorts of Christianity that existed in the British Isles would clash at some point. The Celtic Church had developed in quite a different way from the Roman Church. They believed in the same things, but they organised themselves quite differently. One of the most important differences was that the Celtic Church did not recognise the authority of the Pope in Rome, and in this they were out of step with the rest of the Christian world. The Roman Church was not happy with this. Its members preferred a rigid structure where what people believed and how they behaved was controlled by bishops working in their cathedrals, receiving guidance from the archbishops and Pope above them and passing this guidance on to the priests who worked in the churches in the villages and townships. The Celtic Church, with its loose network of small monasteries, mainly based in the countryside and where the abbot was the 'father' of his flock, seemed to fit in much better with the Saxon way of life, based as it was on family bonds, than the far more bureaucratic Roman approach.

Matters came to a head over, of all things, an argument about the date of Easter. Celtic Christians and Roman Christians used different methods of working out the date and this caused problems, particularly in the Northumbrian court where King Osuiu followed the Celtic practice but his wife followed the Roman ways she had learned as a child in Kent. Of course, the hidden agenda was whether the Celtic or Roman Church should be the one to be accepted throughout Saxon England. The whole matter was fiercely debated at Whitby in 664 – and the Roman side won.

If you look up references to the Synod of Whitby, you will find a lot of material written by the Venerable Bede (but remember he was on the Roman side) and also some paintings like the modern one in Source 20.

- What use can we make of modern paintings like Source 20?
- Now look at Source 21. What sort of society would be able to produce something like this?

● **SOURCE 20**

This is a mural showing the Synod of Whitby. It was painted on a wall in St Hilda's priory, in Whitby, towards the end of the twentieth century.

● **SOURCE 21**

A page from the Lindisfarne Gospels, made by monks in the late seventh or early eighth century.

The rise of Wessex

No single Saxon king was strong enough to gain control of the whole country until the tenth century, though some came very close to doing so.

- In the seventh century the rule of the Northumbrian kings often came almost as far as the River Thames.
- In the eighth century Mercia became the strongest kingdom under Ethelbald (716–57) and Offa (757–96). Offa's Dyke, a great defensive ditch and bank stretching from the River Dee to the Bristol Channel, can still be seen. When he died, Offa was lord of all lands south of the River Humber and east of this dyke. But after his death, the power of Mercia crumbled under attacks from King Egbert of Wessex.
- In the ninth century, Wessex was to emerge as the only kingdom strong enough to withstand the onslaught of the Vikings, as you will see on pages 19–31.

How had this happened?

In 825, sensing weaknesses in the kingdom of Mercia, Egbert of Wessex expelled the Mercian king from Kent, annexing Kent, Essex, Surrey and Sussex. Four years later, Mercia itself and then Northumbria acknowledged the over-lordship of Egbert. Historians believe that two main factors go a long way to explaining why this came about:

1 The West Saxon monarchy became extremely wealthy due to conquering Cornwall with its rich mineral resources.
2 Egbert's family was able to sort out the succession without resorting to in-fighting. Egbert's son Ethelwulf had so organised matters that his own four sons would rule Wessex in turn after his death.

This was just as well. Wessex alone was able to withstand the firestorm of Viking attacks.

Summary task

1 Throughout this section on the Saxons, you have looked at different sorts of evidence. Each sort of evidence has strengths and weaknesses.
   a) List the sorts of evidence and note beside each what its strengths and weaknesses are.
   b) Then devise an interesting way of displaying this information.

2 By now you will have found out a lot about the Saxons as raiders, invaders and settlers. You should be ready to answer the 'big' question:

'Were the Saxons successful raiders and invaders?'

This should be a major piece of writing, in which you bring in hard evidence to back up what you are saying about the Saxons.

The Vikings

The *Anglo-Saxon Chronicle*, a history of the times kept by monks over hundreds of years, made a note that was to prove ominous:

● SOURCE 1

In this year Beorhtric [the King of Wessex] *took to wife Eadburh, daughter of King Offa. And in his days came first three ships of Norwegians from Horthaland: and then the reeve rode thither and tried to compel them to go to the royal manor, for he did not know what they were: and then they slew him. These were the first ships of the Danes to come to England.*

The *Anglo-Saxon Chronicle*, 789.

The first three ships were not the last. The fire-storm was about to begin.

Why did the Vikings first raid, and then invade, the British Isles?

Between 789 and 792 the *Anglo-Saxon Chronicle* refers to 'sea-borne pagans' attacking the south coast of England. No church or monastery within ten miles of the shore was safe from the ravages of the Vikings. But it was the unprotected monasteries in the north that provided the best pickings. The Vikings began to slaughter and plunder on a regular basis. In 793 they attacked Lindisfarne; in 794, Jarrow; and in 795, Iona. All over the country people prayed 'From the fury of the Northmen, good Lord deliver us'.

Terrifying as these raids were to those who experienced them, they were a relatively minor irritation when compared to the huge Viking raid on Kent in 835. It was this raid that started a series of massive attacks on Saxon England, ending in a full-scale invasion thirty years later.

● SOURCE 2

Antony Wootten's reconstruction of a Viking raiding ship (twentieth century).

● SOURCE 3

A photograph of the restored Gokstad ship.

In 1880 the 'Kings Mound' on the Gokstad farm in Sandar, Norway, was excavated and found to contain a Viking ship which was the burial place of a Viking king or lord. Source 3 is a photograph of the ship archaeologists unearthed.

- Look at Sources 2 and 3. In what ways could each source be used to describe Viking raids?

Raiding is perhaps easy to explain. By the 840s the Vikings had been heavily involved in trading for forty to fifty years and had travelled far up the rivers and estuaries of Europe. They would have known about the rich pickings to be had from undefended monasteries and cathedrals throughout western Europe and Russia. It was hardly surprising that some traders turned into raiders.

It's important, however, to see the raids on the British Isles by Norwegians and Danes as part of a wider picture of Viking trading, raiding and invading that took place throughout Europe. It seems to be that, from about the 850s onwards, casual plundering changed into determined invasion and a policy of conquest and settlement. Historians believe that this was because pressure of population growth in Norway and Denmark meant that the land could no longer sustain the number of people who wanted to live on it. Insofar as the British Isles were concerned, there seem to have been two main raiding and invading routes: from Norway around the north of Scotland to the Western Isles, Ireland, Wales and Cornwall, and from Denmark to the east and south coasts of England.

Case study: How did Alfred ensure the survival and prosperity of Wessex?

The West Saxon kingdom of Wessex withstood attacks from the Danes, reached an agreement with the invaders and, by the time of Alfred's death in 899, was a thriving and prosperous kingdom with a reputation for culture and learning. How had this happened?

Survival: the first priority

By late in 870 the Danish 'Great Army', having invaded in force, had wiped out the kingdom of Northumbria, taken York and set up their own puppet ruler; they had overrun East Anglia and were poised to attack Wessex. Everything seemed to be going their way.

But:

- King Ethelwulf had so organised Wessex (look back to page 18) that the kingdom was in a good position to defend itself against the Danes. The lack of family feuds enabled Ethelwulf's third son Aethelred (who was king of Wessex when the Danes attacked) to combine forces with his brother Alfred.
- The respect that the West Saxons had for Ethelwulf's sons meant that they rallied round Alfred when the going was difficult. In 878 Alfred was forced to flee to the comparative safety of the Somerset marshes around Athelney. Read Source 4 to see what happened next.

● SOURCE 4

He rode to Edbert's Stone and there came to meet him all the men of Somerset and Wiltshire and part of Hampshire and they rejoiced to see him. And one day later he went from those camps to Iley Oak and one day later to Edington; and there he fought against the entire host, and put it to flight.

The *Anglo-Saxon Chronicle*, 878.

It was at this point that peace terms were agreed between Alfred and Guthrum, the Danish leader.

- The Danish occupation of much of England was recognised and accepted.
- A frontier between Danish-occupied lands (the Danelaw) and the rest of the British Isles, was agreed.
- Guthrum agreed to withdraw behind this frontier with his troops.
- Alfred recognised Guthrum as king of the independent Danish kingdom to the east of the frontier.
- Guthrum agreed to be baptised a Christian.

By the autumn of 880, the Danes had withdrawn from Wessex and east Mercia and concentrated on settling much of England.

● **SOURCE 5**

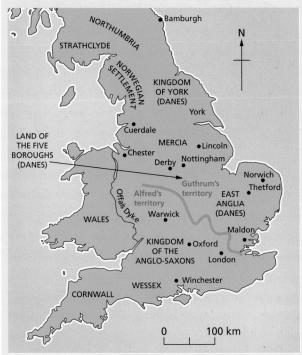

Map to show England at the death of King Alfred, 899.

Discussion point

Had Alfred done anything more than accept what was obvious: the Danish occupation of most of England?

Security: the next priority

The agreement with Guthrum bought Alfred a breathing space. It was a breathing space in which he concentrated on

1. securing the safety of Wessex and
2. consolidating his lordship over lands to the west and south of the Danish frontier.

Read the following list of changes made by Alfred and decide, for each one, which of his aims, 1 or 2, they would have helped him achieve.

- He reorganised his fighting men so that only half of the potential army was on duty at any one time, making for a smaller but more efficient fighting force.
- He commissioned the building of ships bigger than those used by the Vikings.
- He built a series of public strongholds, called burhs, throughout Wessex that were really fortified towns which were maintained by the local landowners.
- He recaptured London (which had once been part of Mercia) and handed it over to Aethelred, a Mercian ealdorman (prince) who was shortly to be allowed to marry Alfred's daughter.
- He became known as a just and considerate king, and so the western Mercians were ready to accept his rule, particularly when his daughter Aethelflaed was married to the Mercian leader Aethelred.

Alfred's changes were put to the test in 892 when a large force of Danes crossed the Channel from France and landed on the Kent coast. Using this as a base, they plundered the Midlands and the south-east. Wessex and most of Alfred's burhs held firm. The Danish force finally split, with some going to live in the Danelaw and the rest returning to France.

... and prosperity

- Look carefully at these artefacts (Sources 6–8) made during Alfred's time. How do they help to show the prosperity of Wessex?
- What other evidence would you need before you could say for certain that Wessex was a prosperous kingdom by the end of Alfred's reign? How would you set about finding it?

● **SOURCE 6**

The Alfred jewel was found in 1963 in the marshes of Athelney. The words around it read 'Alfred had me made' and the jewel itself is made from gold, rock crystal and enamel.

● **SOURCE 7**

The Fuller brooch was made from silver during Alfred's reign. The design shows the five senses. Can you tell which sense is shown in each of the five pictures in the centre?

● **SOURCE 8**

These coins are from the reign of Alfred.

Alfred's legacy

Many of Alfred's burhs developed into prosperous towns. Landowners, who were responsible for their defence, often built 'town houses' in which to store produce for marketing. Merchants, traders and craftsmen followed, together with their workshops, homes and families. The road system laid out in the original burhs survives to this day in towns like Winchester and Wallingford.

The Danes did irreparable damage to the monasteries, abbeys and churches they raided. Monasteries were the centres of learning, and the Vikings destroyed and damaged hundreds of documents, charters and records. It was partly this that drove Alfred to revive literacy and learning. He started a programme of education through a circle of court intellectuals and was the only monarch until Henry VIII who wrote books. He learned Latin and was enthusiastic about translating works into English for his people. His court circle was responsible for translating and preserving Bede's *Ecclesiastical History* and the *Anglo-Saxon Chronicle*.

For what else should we remember Alfred?

● SOURCE 9

This painting by Daniel Maclise (1806–70) shows King Alfred disguised as a minstrel in Guthrum the Dane's tent.

- Look at Source 9. It is entirely imaginary and was based on no known incident. Of what use is it in helping us to understand the importance of King Alfred?

How do we know about the Vikings?

One of the two 'big' questions at the end of the section on the Saxons asked about problems with the evidence of the Saxons in England. The problems with evidence of the Vikings are a bit different.

Contemporary accounts, written by the Vikings themselves, about their raiding and invading of the British Isles, are virtually non-existent. The accounts that we do have are almost all written by churchmen, who condemned Viking raids because they were non-Christian. Indeed, letters from the scholar Alcuin, for example, interpret the Viking raids as God's punishment on the Anglo-Saxons for their sins. Look in the ragbag (page 44) and read what he wrote to Ethelred, King of Northumbria, in 793.

Sagas give us detailed accounts of the Viking age. Although most are about powerful rulers of, for example, Norway and Orkney, some deal with the ordinary people of Iceland. It should be possible to make inferences from these about what happened in Britain. However, the sagas were often written down two or three hundred years after the events they describe and it's not clear what was based in fact and what was invented to make a good story.

Runes are Viking lettering. They were usually carved, not written, and so were used for fairly short inscriptions. This is probably the main reason why we do not have long written accounts from the Vikings. They did not use the Roman alphabet (the one we use today) until they converted to Christianity.

Coins can sometimes be informative. Archaeologists found a coin minted in York around 900. On one side its inscription read *Ebraice* (a version of the Latin name for York); on the other side, it read *CNUT REX* (King Cnut). Without this coin we would have no idea that a King Cnut ran York, although we do know that someone called Cnut was raiding at that time.

Evidence from archaeological digs

- In Norway, a Viking woman's grave was found to contain a small wooden bucket and ladle. The decorations on the bucket were Northumbrian and dated from the 700s.
- On the Orkney Islands, it was common for archaeologists to find combs made from deer antlers by the native Picts, and combs made by the Vikings, which were made from reindeer antlers. Archaeologists knew which were which because of the carvings. Then they dug up combs made from reindeer antlers but with Pictish carvings on them.

Discussion point

What possible explanations could there be for the Saxon bucket (made long before the *Anglo-Saxon Chronicle* recorded the first Viking raids on Britain) that was found in the Viking grave, and the reindeer antler combs with Pictish carvings on them when there were no reindeer on the Orkney Islands?

The following were found on Anglesey:

- Ninth-century coins and small lead weights used by Viking traders.
- Five beautifully decorated Viking silver arm bands.
- A ninth-century defensive wall, made from massive stone blocks and about 2 metres wide at its base.
- Five skeletons, dating from the ninth century, that had been just thrown into a ditch and not buried with any ceremony at all. One of them was of a young male with his hands tied behind his back.

● **SOURCE 10**

The Cuerdale Hoard.

Discussion point

What had happened here? Construct an explanation for the archaeological finds on Anglesey.

The Cuerdale Hoard is the largest hoard of Viking silver ever found in Western Europe. It contained about 8,600 items of coins and bullion, armbands and brooches, chains and buckles. It was found in 1840 by workmen repairing the embankment on the south side of the River Ribble at Cuerdale, near Preston in Lancashire. Coins found with the hoard revealed that it must have been buried sometime between 905 and 910.

What was this massive amount of treasure doing buried in a riverbank in Lancashire? There are three facts that may help here. In 902 the Vikings were expelled from Dublin. The new coins in the hoard were minted in York. The valley of the River Ribble was the main route between Viking York and the Irish Sea. Can you come up with an explanation?

How well did the Vikings settle the Danelaw?

We now use the word 'Danelaw' to mean the huge area of land in the east and north-east of Britain that Alfred and Guthrum agreed should be under Danish control, even though the name didn't appear in legal documents until 1008. But the name itself doesn't give us any indication of how the Danes controlled the region, nor of what the native Saxons thought of their new rulers. Part of the problem is the old one: that early chronicles tend to focus on what the chroniclers (usually monks) thought were important events. So Alfred's battles are seen as important, but the scale of the Viking settlement isn't. Even when the *Anglo-Saxon Chronicle* reports that the Danes divided up the land amongst themselves, it doesn't give us any details as to how this was done. We have to deduce what happened from the evidence that remains.

Where did the Vikings settle?

Place names are a major piece of evidence for Viking settlement of the Danelaw. The ending *-by* usually indicates a homestead. So there is Grimsby (Grim's homestead) Thurnby (homestead near a thorn bush) and Derby (village near the deer). From this we can work out that Derby and Thurnby were probably agricultural villages, whereas Grimsby, from its position on the coast, was possibly much as it is today – a place of fishing and trade. The ending *-thorpe* is Viking, too, and means 'a new village' (think about Scunthorpe – Skuma's village); *-thwaite* is a Viking word meaning 'meadow' or 'piece of land'.

Task

Use a modern atlas and find all the places in the old Danelaw that end with *-by*, *-thorpe* and *-thwaite*. What conclusions can you draw from what you have found out?

● **SOURCE 11**

Freydis, My Lady, talking to her 'villagers' in the long house at the end of the day

You may have found, as some historians have done, that in the region called the 'Five Boroughs' (Derby, Leicester, Lincoln, Nottingham and Stamford) where most of the Vikings seem to have settled, there are a lot of place names ending in *-by* that include a person's name. In fact, 68 per cent of the places are named like this, as opposed to only 10 per cent in Denmark. Maybe this was where individual members of the Great Army settled and named their original homesteads after themselves. Certainly the 'Five Boroughs' were strongly fortified towns and the name 'borough' links back to the Saxon 'burh' (see page 21).

The photograph in Source 11 was taken at the Danelaw village at Murton Park in Yorkshire. The village is a reconstruction of one that might have been built by the Vikings living in the Danelaw. Schoolchildren can go along and become Vikings (or Saxons) for the day. They learn about what everyday life would have been like in the village.

- How useful are reconstructed villages like this in helping us understand what everyday life was like in the Danelaw?

How adaptable were the Vikings?

We can learn a lot from what archaeologists call **material culture**. This is a phrase that refers simply to the stuff that Vikings had with them: bowls and brooches, pottery and pins. In the Danelaw, archaeologists have found silk from Byzantium and pottery from the Shetland Islands and the Rhineland. It would seem that the Vikings took what they liked from the peoples with whom they were in contact. Look in the ragbag and see what the archaeologist Julian Richards has to say about this.

It would seem that the Saxons living in the Danelaw began to adopt the fashions and customs of the Viking settlers. They had no reason not to: they owed no loyalty to Wessex and may just as easily have found themselves threatened by Wessex's plans to expand as by the Vikings' plans to invade.

The Vikings seemed pretty flexible, too. For example, in the early years of the Danelaw the Vikings didn't mint coins. Payment was by weight and the Vikings used any bit of silver that was appropriate. A brooch was just as much use to them, for example, as a silver coin. But they allowed the East Anglians to mint coins and use them as currency. Several mints produced coins in the name of St Edmund the King. On the one hand this might have seemed a bit odd, as the Vikings had themselves killed the East Anglian King Edmund (thus turning him into an almost instant saint) and it might seem strange that they would allow coins commemorating this man to be circulated. But it might have been a canny move. It was possible that the Danes anticipated trouble from the East Anglians after the death of the Viking leader Guthrum in 890. A martyred king would be a wonderful rallying point for the East Anglians. But by acknowledging King Edmund's martyrdom in allowing the coins to be circulated, the Vikings were defusing the situation.

- Look at Sources 12 and 13. Would you say, based on the evidence of these two crosses, that the Vikings were Christians?

SOURCE 12

How did the Vikings administer the Danelaw?

The Danelaw was not one uniformly administered area so it is very difficult to make any generalisations about how it was run. It's probably clearer to take an example, and a good one to use here is the huge area that now forms Yorkshire. Here, for ease of administration, the Viking rulers divided the land into three separate units. The Viking word for a third of something was *thrithjungr*. This was later modified to 'Riding' and until 1974 Yorkshire was divided into the East, West and North Ridings. Within the thrithjungr came the *vapnatak* (or wapentake) and it was at meetings of this local parliament and court that freemen voted by a show of weapons that were then counted.

Were the Vikings Christians?

You read earlier about the Viking raids on churches and monasteries. But these seem to be far more raids in search of treasure than anything anti-Christian. It just so happened that the treasure was kept in religious buildings. Certainly Guthrum was more than prepared to be baptised a Christian, as were several of his captains.

This stone cross was found in St Andrew's Church in Middleton, North Yorkshire. Some archaeologists think the man under the cross is a pagan warrior stretched out in his grave with his weapons. Others think the figure is of a warrior on a throne. Either way, it is very unusual, in standard Christian carvings, to have a warrior and a cross together. The cross was made in the ninth or tenth century.

● SOURCE 13

This huge stone cross is in the churchyard at Gosforth, Cumbria. The cross at the top is Viking in style, but the carvings around the sides of the cross are a mixture of scenes from the Christian Bible and the Danish saga Ragnarok. Ragnarok describes the end of the world, when pagan gods are overthrown by the forces of evil.

Viking York

The best evidence of the ways in which the Vikings lived comes from the city of York. The Vikings captured York in 866 and held on to it despite the desperate attempts by the Northumbrians to take the city back the following year. It was the Viking takeover of the kingdom of Northumbria, and later the Danelaw, that confirmed the importance of Viking York, turning the city into a thriving, bustling international trading centre.

Between 1976 and 1981 the York Archaeological Trust carried out a massive archaeological excavation at Coppergate that revealed Viking York in astounding detail.

● SOURCE 14

A photograph of Coppergate excavations.

The archaeologists were lucky. The soil in York provided exactly the right environment for preserving all the objects lost or left behind by York's Viking inhabitants. What the archaeologists dug up amazed them. Twigs and thatch, straw and silver, cups and coins, beads and bedding – it was all there.

Archaeologists were able to work out that by the end of the tenth century, simple wattle and daub houses had been replaced by solid, two-storey timber buildings; behind the houses were workshops built just as strongly from squared oak posts and oak planks. The workshops revealed evidence of many different craftsmen: textile workers, jewellery makers, silversmiths and wood workers. Crucibles and various moulds for working gold, silver, copper and alloys were found, too. The raw materials came not just from Britain, but also from northern Europe, Norway, Denmark and Sweden.

Behind the workshops were wells, latrines and rubbish pits. There, archaeologists found combs with the remains of head lice trapped between the teeth, broken pots and pans, chipped bowls and broken necklaces. From the latrines they could work out what people ate and even found long strips of moss and cloth – Viking toilet paper!

In around 1000, a monk described York as: 'A place enriched with the treasure of merchants who come from all quarters, particularly from the Danish people.'

● **SOURCE 15**

A modern reconstruction by Victor Ambrus of a street in Viking York in the late tenth century. The artist based his drawing on archaeological excavations.

Task

1 Sources 15 and 16 are reconstructions. Would one be of any more use than the other in helping to find out how the Vikings lived in York?

2 Use the internet to find out more about the Jorvik Centre. Can it help develop people's understanding of the York Vikings?

3 If you can, visit the Jorvik Centre. How far does it match up to what you think Viking York was like?

● SOURCE 16

A photograph of the reconstruction of a Viking family's home, which is in the Jorvik Centre, York. The Jorvik Centre is a tourist attraction. It consists of a re-creation by the York Archaeological Trust of a part of York as it would have been in 975, based on the archaeological excavations carried out in the 1970s.

What was the significance of Danegeld and the reign of King Cnut?

● SOURCE 17

980 Southampton was ransacked by a naval force, and most of the citizens killed or taken captive; and in the same year Thanet was ravaged.

981 Great damage was done everywhere along the coast both in Devon and Cornwall.

982 Three ships of Vikings arrived in Dorset and ravaged in Portland. That same year, London was burnt down.

The *Anglo-Saxon Chronicle*, towards the end of the 900s.

Look at Source 17. What was happening here? Was history repeating itself? Were there to be yet more Viking invasions? Yes – and they were to be more violent and more dangerous than ever before.

From Danegeld to the crown

The king at the time was Aethelred. His nickname was Unraed and down through the ages, this has been translated as 'the Unready', although its original meaning was 'no counsel'. It is more than probable that he did lack wise guidance and advice, but he was probably outwitted by circumstances too. By the time Aethelred began his reign in 978, the Danelaw had been absorbed into Wessex and Mercia, and the Wessex kings had with reasonable confidence reigned over all of England south of the River Humber. This was a pretty strong kingdom – or so it seemed. But the Viking invasions exposed its weakness and the folly of trying to pay off invaders.

The first Viking attacks were nothing but small raids. But in 991, large, well-organised and heavily armed Danish warriors wiped out the English force at Maldon, in Essex. Aethelred raised extra taxes from his landowners and paid off the invaders. This tax was called Danegeld. The pattern was repeated again and again after heavy raids in 994, 997 and 1002. What was Aethelred up to? Did he really think he could keep this up for ever?

There is a clue here:

● **SOURCE 18**

When the enemy were in the east, the English army was kept in the west, and when they were in the south, our army was in the north. Finally there was no leader willing to collect an army, but each fled as best he could.

The *Anglo-Saxon Chronicle*, 1002.

Aethelred was struggling to hold things together. He had inherited a powerful, well-established aristocracy and his early charters show that he was building up support with grants of land, just as previous kings of Wessex had done. But nothing could have prepared him for this. As the Viking threat became more severe, it exposed a basic weakness in royal power. The king's lands, and therefore his power, were concentrated in Wessex. His ability to buy support in the north and east were limited – and it was here that he needed support the most. The strain on the government was enormous, and showed when in 1002 Aethelred ordered a massacre of all Danes living in England.

We don't know how thoroughly this was carried out. We do know that there were instances of terrible massacres taking place. In Oxford, for example, Danes took refuge inside St Frideswide's minster church and the citizens burned it down. We know, too, that it was this massacre that prompted King Swein of Denmark to head up a full-scale invasion. Burning and raiding, the Vikings rampaged through Berkshire, Wiltshire and Hampshire; in 1009 they torched Oxford and moved on into East Anglia. Finally, in 1013, Swein returned with the intention of conquest. The people of the old Danelaw accepted him immediately. By the end of the year he had taken Oxford, Winchester and London but died in 1014. The following year, Swein's son, Cnut, returned with an even larger force. He recovered Northumbria and moved towards London. But before the Danes could arrive, Aethelred was dead and his son Edmund had been proclaimed king. It made no difference. Even in Wessex many people accepted Cnut without a struggle and when Edmund died Cnut became king of all England.

Discussion point

Think back through the events that led to Cnut becoming King of England. Start with Danegeld. Was this a mistake? Could Aethelred have played things any differently?

What kind of a king was Cnut?

King Cnut (1016–35), sometimes known as Canute, acted ruthlessly to secure the throne, marrying Aethelred's widow and killing several leading English barons. Once he felt secure, Cnut set about behaving as any other king of Wessex – or of England – would. He issued laws, founded monasteries and rewarded his loyal supporters. One chronicler reported that he *'changed from a wild man into a most Christian king.'*

But Cnut was not just king of England. On his brother's death in 1019 he inherited a vast northern empire of which Britain was only a small part. It was Cnut's need to be away from England for long stretches of time that led him to make changes that were to have long-term significance:

- Although there was no wholesale removal of existing landowners, as there was to be after the Norman takeover, many Danes joined the existing English landowning class.
- Cnut kept a regiment of Danish household troops – or housecarls – as his personal bodyguard. Now, instead of paying the Danes to keep away, the landowners were paying to support a Danish standing army.
- In order to make English government function while he was away, Cnut divided the kingdom into four earldoms: Northumbria, East Anglia, Mercia and Wessex.

By the end of King Cnut's reign in 1035, the three most important men in the kingdom were Siward, Earl of Northumbria; Leofric, Earl of Mercia and, fatefully, Godwine, Earl of Wessex.

- Which of Cnut's changes do you think was the most potentially dangerous to the security of his realm and his position as ruler? Why?

Summary task

1 Do the problems with the evidence about the Vikings mean that we know more about the Saxons?

2 By this point you have found out a lot about the Vikings. You should now be ready to write a substantial piece of work about them.

'The Vikings were a warlike people who were much better at raiding and invading than they were at settling.'

How far would you agree with this view?

Remember to bring in as much evidence as you can to support what you say and do not make sweeping generalisations that cannot be backed up by evidence.

Invasion!

● SOURCE 1

● SOURCE 2

- Look at Sources 1–3. What is happening here? Describe what you see. Forget anything you may know about these images. Write down just what you can see and what conclusions you can draw from what you see.

● SOURCE 3

Did you say that there was an invasion going on? If you did, you will need to be very careful. How do you *know*, from these images, that this is what was happening? Ships are being built, sailing somewhere with men and horses, and then disembarking. That an invasion was happening may have been a reasonable conclusion, but you need more evidence to be really sure.

- Look at Source 4. Now can you be sure? Why?

● SOURCE 4

Why did the Normans invade England in 1066?

A Norman writer tells of a message sent from King Edward of England to Duke William of Normandy:

● SOURCE 5

Edward, king of the English, according to the dispensation of God, without an heir, sent Robert, Archbishop of Canterbury, to the duke with a message appointing the duke as heir to the kingdom which God had entrusted him.

William of Jumièges, 1070s.

Another Norman writing at the same time seems to give us a very strong steer. In Source 6 he is writing about a meeting between Duke William of Normandy and Harold Godwinsson, Earl of Wessex. At the time of the meeting, Harold was the most powerful man in England apart from King Edward, and could reasonably hope to succeed him.

● SOURCE 6

When they had come together in conference at Bonneville, Harold in that place swore loyalty to the duke. And as is testified by the most truthful and most honourable men who were there present, he took an oath of his own free will in the following terms: firstly that he would be the representative of Duke William at the court of his lord, King Edward, as long as the king lived; secondly that he would employ all his influence and wealth to ensure that after the death of King Edward the kingdom of England should be confirmed in the possession of the Duke.

William of Poitiers, 1070s.

The Bayeux Tapestry was made on the orders of Odo, Bishop of Bayeux and half-brother of Duke William of Normandy.

● SOURCE 7

Harold making an oath to Duke William.

• Use Sources 5–8 to explain what you think has been happening. Can you be sure?

Did the dying King Edward offer the throne of England to Harold Godwinsson? The Bayeux Tapestry (Source 8) certainly shows the dying Edward touching hands with someone, but can we be sure it was Harold?

● SOURCE 8

Edward the Confessor on his deathbed.

Maybe written sources can help here.

● SOURCE 9

Harold knows that this kingdom is his by right, as granted to him by gift of that same king his lord Edward upon his deathbed. For since the time when the blessed Augustine came into England it has been the common custom of this nation that a gift made at the point of death is held as valid.

This is what the Norman, William of Poitiers, writing in 1070, has to say.

What about English sources? By this time there were five different versions of the *Anglo-Saxon Chronicle*, written by different monks across the country.

● SOURCE 10

C version: *Yet did the wise king entrust his kingdom to a man of high rank, to Harold himself.*

E version: *King Harold succeeded to the kingdom of England as the king granted it to him and he was elected thereto.*

This is what two of them have as entries for 1066.

Harold was crowned King of England in Westminster Abbey on 6 January 1066. At the same time, and in the same place, the old king, Edward the Confessor, was buried. Whether or not Edward had promised anything to Harold, it seems clear that the assembled nobility and clergy were content with the outcome. Harold had popular support and, probably, the agreement of his predecessor. Nothing more was needed. What did an oath matter if it was made a couple of years earlier, may or may not have been about the succession to the English throne and may or may not have been made under duress? As it happened, it mattered very much indeed.

Discussion point

We know the Normans invaded England in 1066. How helpful are Sources 9 and 10 as evidence of their reasons for doing this?

Why was the Norman invasion successful?

In the short term, we know that the invasion of 1066 was successful. Both Norman and English sources tell us so:

● SOURCE 11

Realising that they could not, without severe loss, overcome an army massed so strongly in close formation, the Normans and their allies feigned flight and simulated a retreat. The barbarians [English], thinking victory within their grasp, shouted with triumph. They gave rapid pursuit to those who they thought to be in flight. But the Normans, suddenly wheeling their horses, surrounded them and cut down their pursuers so that not one was left alive. Twice was this tactic employed, with the greatest success.

William of Poitiers.

● SOURCE 12

King Harold assembled a large army and came against him at the hoary apple tree. But William took him by surprise before his army was drawn up in battle array. But the King nevertheless fought hard against him, with the men who were willing to support him, and there were heavy casualties on both sides. There King Harold was killed and Earl Leofwine his brother, and Earl Gyrth his brother and many good men. The French remained masters of the field, even as God granted it to them because of the sins of the people.

The D version of the *Anglo-Saxon Chronicle*.

- How do the two accounts (Sources 11 and 12) differ in the reasons they give for the Norman victory?
- Have we any reason to trust one account more than the other?

Source 13 shows how axes, knives and swords were used in hand-to-hand fighting. The heavy, two-handed axe was a frightening weapon, but in order to use it effectively, the soldier had to sling his shield over his back so as to leave both arms free.

● **SOURCE 13**

A re-enactment of the Battle of Hastings.

- Do re-enactments of the Battle of Hastings show it is still significant today?

The Battle of Hastings was the only pitched battle fought by the Saxons to try to prevent the Norman invasion. Harold Godwinsson was killed along with his brothers Leofwine and Gyrth. Although the Normans had to work hard to establish themselves in England, they never again had to face serious, organised, Saxon opposition. How was it that Hastings had been so successful?

- **William's preparations**   William had prepared well. His army was superbly fit and well equipped. He shipped over hundreds of horses and archers in specially designed ships. He even brought with him prefabricated wooden castles.
- **Harold's circumstances**   Harold was expecting two invasions: from Harald Hardrada in the north and from William of Normandy in the south. This put tremendous strain on his resources. He had, for example, to keep his armies mobilised from May through to September. He managed to put down Hardrada's invasion with speed and skill on 20 September, massacring the invaders outside York at the Battle of Stamford Bridge, even though his brother Tostig was killed. When Harold and William met at Hastings, their armies were equal in size.
- **Harold's mistakes**   Harold could have waited. His men were exhausted after the battle of Stamford Bridge and the long march south. Edwin and Morcar, his loyal brothers-in-law, were marching south with fresh troops. Harold had no need to fight when he did.
- **Generalship**   William was the better general. He wasn't afraid to try out new tactics – like pretending to retreat. Harold was used to fighting straightforward pitched battles and had no idea how to outwit William.
- **Luck**   The wind changed for William at exactly the right moment, enabling him to cross the Channel just when Harold and his army were at their most vulnerable.
- **God**   William used what he saw as Harold's oath-breaking as a reason for enlisting the Pope's support for his invasion of England. The psychological advantage of this was enormous because most people at the time believed that it was God who granted victory in battle.

Discussion point

In your view, was any one factor more important than the others in ensuring a successful invasion for the Normans?

How well did the Normans establish control?

Winning the Battle of Hastings was one thing. Establishing Norman rule throughout England was quite another. William began as he meant to go on. Slashing and burning, ruthlessly putting down opposition, he marched on London. Even during his coronation in Westminster Abbey on Christmas Day 1066, there was hand-to-hand fighting between Saxons and Normans in the streets of London. Not an auspicious beginning.

In the years 1067 to 1071 a series of revolts threatened the very existence of the new regime. Each one was put down with great brutality, ending any pretence that William was the legitimate heir of Edward the Confessor.

Putting down rebellions

Rebellions broke out across all England:

The South-West 1068 The city of Exeter refused to accept William's rule and held out against a Norman siege for eighteen days. William installed his half-brother Robert of Mortain as Earl of Cornwall and forced Bristol and Gloucester to submit to him.

The North 1069–70 The Saxon leaders who remained – Edwin, Morcar and Edgar Aethling – fled north during 1068. Raising a huge force (remember, the North had always been separatist and semi-independent) they burned the Norman bishop Robert of Commines in his bishop's house in Durham and marched on York. Then the Vikings, never far away, intervened. A fleet of 240 ships sailed up the River Humber and Viking warriors fought with the Saxons against the Normans, managing in the end to seize York. Malcolm, King of Scotland, promptly married Edgar Aethling's sister, Margaret. William was now faced with the very real prospect of a separate Scandinavian kingdom in northern England.

What would William do? The answer was simple. He responded in the only way he knew how.

Harrying of the North is a phrase used by historians to describe a revenge so terrible that chroniclers, writing about it fifty years later, couldn't hide their horror. One of these was the chronicler Orderic Vitalis. Read William's deathbed confession in Source 14. William marched north with crack troops; he burned York and set about the destruction of Yorkshire itself. Men, women and children were massacred, their bodies left to rot where they died. Where the people could flee, they did; those who survived faced famine as the Normans fired their homes and fields and slaughtered their animals. If famine didn't kill those who remained, disease did. The Danes, seeing their Saxon allies defeated, sailed away.

East Anglia 1070–71 England wasn't quite subdued. In the Fens of East Anglia, Edwin, Morcar and a thegn called Hereward made one last stand. Together with King Swein of Denmark and a sizeable Danish force, they attacked Peterborough Cathedral, sacked it and made off with much treasure. It wasn't, in the end, much of a rebellion. William bought off the Danes, who left. With a Norman army advancing on Ely, the monks, anxious to retain their lands, betrayed the Saxons. Morcar surrendered to William; Edwin fled and was later murdered; and Hereward simply disappeared.

● SOURCE 14

I fell on the English of the northern shires like a ravening lion. I commanded their houses and corn, with all their implements and chattels, to be burned without distinction, and large herds of cattle and beasts of burden to be butchered wherever they were found. And by so doing, alas, I became the barbarous murderer of many thousands, both young and old, of that fine race of people.

William's deathbed confession, recorded by a chronicler Orderic Vitalis writing between 1123 and 1141. William died in 1087.

● SOURCE 15

A nineteenth-century drawing showing Hereward the Wake attacking the Normans.

Look at Sources 14 and 15.

- How problematical are these sources for someone trying to find out about the Normans?
- How could both sources be used to show the Normans' importance?

● SOURCE 16

This painting by Simon Hayfield is of the first Norman castle built at Pickering in North Yorkshire.

Building castles

It was over. In less than ten years the Normans had subdued Saxon England. But how could they keep control? One of the answers was by building castles. Before the time of William I, castles were virtually unheard of and unseen in England. True, the Romans had built large fortresses and the Saxons had built burhs, but neither of these were castles in the Norman sense of the word.

- Look at this reconstruction of one of the first Norman castles. What, just looking at the reconstruction, was it for?

● **SOURCE 17**

He then went to Nottingham and built a castle there, so from there to York, and there built castles, also in Lincoln and elsewhere in those parts. He built castles widely throughout this nation and oppressed the people wretchedly and afterwards it grew much more evil.

An entry from the *Anglo-Saxon Chronicle* for 1067.

• How far do these written sources support what you said castles were for?

● **SOURCE 18**

They [the Normans] filled the whole land with these castles. They burdened the unhappy people of the country with forced labour on the castles. And when the castles were made, they filled them with wicked men.

An entry from the *Anglo-Saxon Chronicle* in 1137.

William built hundreds of castles throughout England. He had even brought pre-fabricated ones with him from Normandy and they proved useful refuges on his march to London. The first castles were built from wood and, although most were eventually replaced by stone, a well-built and well-maintained wooden castle could last for up to 200 years.

So, to return to the first question: what were castles for? They were obviously useful refuges for soldiers and storage places for weapons and ammunition. But they were far more than that. Castles controlled the countryside surrounding them: forests, fields, port, river crossing or border; they were a visible, and therefore psychological reminder of the conquest and of which group of people was in charge. Indeed, it was William's habit to build castles in the middle of large towns that involved pulling down hundreds of houses. Lincoln, Gloucester, Oxford and Cambridge, for example, lost houses in this way. What point was William trying to make?

Many of William's castles later became substantial centres of local administration, of tax collection and of ensuring that Norman laws were upheld. It was obviously essential that castles were run by people in whom William had absolute trust.

Discussion point

Was William's castle-building programme a sign of strength or weakness?

What was the impact of the Normans on the government of England?

Probably the best evidence for the impact the Normans had on the way England was governed comes from the Domesday Book, a survey completed in 1086. The immediate trigger for the Domesday survey seems to have been the threat of yet another Danish invasion, which did not, in fact, materialise.

Domesday is a rich source, and is particularly useful because from it we can learn how land ownership and land use changed from the time of Edward the Confessor (pre-1066) to 1085/6 when the survey was compiled. By looking at land ownership, we are on the way to working out what the impact of the Normans was on the old Saxon system of government.

● **SOURCE 19**

In the city of York, before 1066 were 6 shires besides the Archbishop's. One of these has been laid waste for the castles. In 5 shires there were 1418 inhabited dwellings. Out of the aforementioned dwellings there are now inhabited, and paying customary dues, 400 less 9, both large and small; 400 dwellings not inhabited of which the better ones pay 1 penny and the others less; and 540 dwellings so empty that they pay nothing at all; and the Frenchmen hold 145 dwellings.

Ralph holds Langelei from the Count [Count Robert of Mortain, half brother of William 1]. It answers for 1.5 hides. Land for 16 ploughs. 1 Frenchman with 4 villagers and 5 smallholders have 2 ploughs; 12 ploughs possible. 2 mills at 16 shillings; 2 slaves; meadow for 3 ploughs; pasture for the livestock; woodland; 240 pigs. Total value 40 shillings; when acquired £4; before 1066 £8. Thorir and Seric, two of Earl Leofwine's men, held this manor.

In this manor [at Thetford] there used to be a market on Saturdays. But William Malet [William's Chamberlain] made his castle at Eye, and he made another market in his castle on Saturdays, and thereby the bishop's market has been so far spoilt that it was of little value.

Extracts from the Domesday Book.

- How had land use in these three areas of England changed after the Conquest?
- How had land ownership changed in these three areas after the Conquest?
- Would you expect to find these changes throughout the country? How could you check?

It seems clear that by 1100 the entire Saxon ruling class – earls, bishops and thegns – had been replaced by Normans. But how far had the Saxon system of government changed?

- Under Edward the Confessor a body of royal clerks worked in the royal **chancery**, writing up official documents. One man, the **chancellor**, was in charge, and was responsible for the royal seal. This kind of arrangement was unheard of in Normandy. William took it over and established Norman chancellors. But there was not a lot of point in writing out royal instructions, writs and laws if they couldn't be translated into action out in the country.
- By the time of Edward the Confessor, England was divided into administrative **shires**, with a **sheriff** in each shire being responsible for making sure the King's will was carried out there. It was a system that worked, and William saw no reason to change it. He simply replaced Saxon sheriffs with Norman appointees.
- The most important law courts under Edward were the **shire courts** that met twice a year to hear and decide important cases and were attended by all the great landowners of the shire. Nothing like this existed in Normandy but, again, it was a system that worked and William saw no need to change it. Eventually, all the great landowners were Norman, anyway. It was the same with the **hundred courts**. The old Saxon division of shires into hundreds continued unchanged into Norman times and it was these hundred courts that heard and decided most of the day-to-day disputes, and continued to do so. The old system of trial by ordeal continued but was increasingly replaced by decisions of a jury.

- The Saxons had developed a system of taxation that was based on the **geld** and the Danegeld, a geld paid to keep the Danes away (look back to page 29). Traditionally, the king and his advisers decided each year on the size of the geld that was needed to run the country, and apportioned it amongst the shires. Again, William saw no need to change this system that so obviously worked. Coinage could only be made in royal mints and William, as king, quickly took control of them.

William made no changes to the Saxon system of government, except for making sure it was run by Normans. It wasn't simply that the old system worked, although that had a lot to do with it. William, although he had won England by conquest, was anxious to show that he was, in fact, the true heir to Edward the Confessor and so he couldn't be seen to change too much – he had to make sure there was more continuity than change in the ways in which the Normans governed England.

William did, however, introduce two laws that had never before been heard of in England. These were:

- **The Forest Laws** protected William's hunting. Deer, boar and the vegetation they ate became protected and there were severe punishments for poaching. Huge areas of England were forest; William increased the forested area of the country by creating the New Forest in Hampshire, destroying several villages to do so.
- A **Murdrum Fine** was imposed on any hundred where a Norman was murdered and the killer had not been caught.

Discussion point

Which of these changes would have the greatest impact on Saxon society? Why?

What impact did the Normans have on English society?

We have seen how the Normans kept the structures of Saxon government more or less unchanged, except for the people who were running it. Here Normans replaced Saxons. But what the Normans did bring with them was a very different sort of social structure.

Who owned the land?

Sources 20 and 21 describe what happened.

● **SOURCE 20**

An illustration, from about 1400, showing William giving land to his son-in-law, Alan of Brittany. The land has been taken from the English Earl of Mercia.

● SOURCE 21

The King

Gives lots of land to...

give loyalty and soldiers to...

give some land to...

give soldiers and money to...

Norman Lords and Churchmen

give a house and garden to...

work for and give rent to...

Norman and English Knights and Earls

Peasants Tenants

A diagram setting out the Norman feudal system.

- How could Sources 20 and 21 be used to explain the Norman land-holding system?
- In what ways was it different from the Saxon system? (Look back to pages 8–9.)
- In 1100, 90 per cent of people lived in villages and farmed the land. In what ways might the new Norman system have changed the lives of these people? How could you find out?

What happened to the Church?

The Normans behaved towards the Church in much the same way that they behaved towards other Saxon institutions. English bishops and abbots were replaced by French ones, and there was some tinkering with Church organisation. Some of the English dioceses were changed; new cathedrals, abbeys and monasteries were built in the Norman style and with Normans at their head. All in all, a more hierarchical structure was created but at the bottom, unchanged, was the village parish priest.

● SOURCE 22

This painting by Ivan Lapper shows William I's son, William Rufus, inspecting stonework being carved for the nave of a new church. With him are the Archbishop of Canterbury and the master mason. William I commissioned the building of an abbey at Battle in Sussex as a penance for the slaughter that had led to his victory over Harold in 1066.

- How far does this painting help explain the Normans' attitude to the Church in England?

Research task

The Normans in Wales

You now know a lot about the Normans in England, but what about Wales? Did the Normans behave in the same way there? How are you going to find out?

One way, of course, would be to type 'Normans in Wales' into whatever search engine you use. A lot of sites would come up, from Saga holidays and pubs through to plumbers and poodle parlours. You would waste a lot of time checking each one out. These might be good sites to begin with:

www.bbc.co.uk/wales/storyofwelsh/content/thenormans.shtml
Lively, informative and with useful links.

www.castlewales.com/norman.html
A good opening page with some excellent links.

www.bbc.co.uk/wales/nature/sites/naturalhistoryofwales/
Focused on nature, but some interesting information you don't get anywhere else.

www.britainexpress.com/wales/history/marcher-lords.htm
Basically a tourist guide, but 'The Norman Invasion of Wales' is a useful page.

www.globusz.com/ebooks/Wales/00000018.htm
Chapter VII of an ebook – full and informative.

But if you are going to read an e-book, why not try real ones? Look in your library for books on Norman or early medieval history. Use the index of the first one to find what information there is in it on Wales and make notes. Then develop these by using the index of the second book – and so on until you have a complete set of notes on the Normans in Wales. You'll need to cross-reference between the books as you will between internet sites and work out what really happened.

You could mix internet sites with real books!

Now you should have enough information to answer the question:

How far was the Norman settlement of Wales different from the Norman settlement of England?

Summary task

1 In what ways was the Norman invasion different from the Viking invasions?

2 How did the ways in which the Normans settled differ from the ways in which the Saxons settled?

A ragbag of sources

● SOURCE 1

In that time the Saxons grew strong by virtue of their large number and increased power in Britain. Hengist having died, however, his son Octha crossed from the northern part of Britain to the kingdom of Kent and from him are descended the kings of Kent. Then Arthur along with the kings of Britain fought against them in those days, but Arthur himself was the military commander ... The twelfth battle was on Mount Badon on which there fell in one day 960 men from one charge by Arthur, and no one struck them down but Arthur himself, as in all the wars he emerged as victor. While they were being defeated in all the battles, the Saxons were seeking help from Germany and their numbers were increased many times over without interruption.

Nennius was writing somewhere around 800. His writings are the first to mention Arthur, but these can't be relied upon as he was a very inventive writer. However, we can't ignore him because he used fifth-century documents that have now been lost.

● SOURCE 2

A modern photograph of a re-enactment of the attack in 491 by the Saxon King Aella on the Romano-British fort of Anderida (Pevensey Castle).

● SOURCE 3

This is how the present life of man on earth, King, appears to me in comparison with that time which is unknown to us. You are sitting feasting with your ealdormen and thegns in winter time; the fire is burning on the hearth in the middle of the hall and all inside is warm, while outside the wintry storms of rain and snow are raging; and a sparrow flies swiftly through the hall. It enters in at one door and quickly flies out through the other. For the few moments it is inside, the storm and wintry tempest cannot touch it, but after the briefest moment of calm, it flits from your sight, out of the wintry storm and into it again. So this life of man appears but for a moment; what follows or indeed what went before, we know not at all.

The Venerable Bede, writing in the 730s, tells a story about King Eadwine and his conversion to Christianity. This is part of what a nobleman says to his king.

● SOURCE 4

But there was more to early Anglo-Saxon society than warfare, savage loyalties and ostentatious splendour. In some ways this was a surprisingly ordered world. The institutions which made the English state so exceptionally strong in the central Middle Ages have their roots in the seventh century or even earlier: the efficiency of 'local government' was one important reason why new overlords could establish power so quickly. The kingdoms seem to have been sub-divided into coherent administrative districts, great blocks of 50 to 100 square miles. To a central settlement, the inhabitants of each district would have looked for justice, and there they would have paid their dues and other public burdens in accordance with a complex system of assessment.

A historian, John Blair, explains the lasting impact of Saxon society.

● **SOURCE 5**

www.bbc.co.uk/history/ancient/anglo_saxons
A lot of source material with information written by specialists.

www.brown.edu/Departments/Medieval_Studies/anglos.html
An excellent site with lots of information and a wide range of sources.

www.pastperfect.info/sites/yeavering/index.html
Archaeological exploration of a recently discovered royal Saxon palace at Yeavering in Northumberland.

www.regia.org
A re-enactment society that gives lots of information about Saxon life and the ways in which this is interpreted.

www.bedesworld.co.uk/
Provides a fascinating insight into Christian life in Saxon England.

There are literally hundreds of websites dealing with different aspects of Anglo-Saxon life. Some have been suggested to you in the text. These are a selection of ones that you should find useful and interesting.

● **SOURCE 6**

Lo, it is nearly 350 years that we and our fathers have inhabited this most lovely land, and never before has such terror appeared in Britain … nor was it thought that such an inroad from the sea could be made. Behold the church of St Cuthbert spattered with the blood of the priests of God, despoiled of all its ornaments; a place more venerable than all in Britain is given as a prey to pagan peoples.
[Alcuin blames the Saxons for what was happening:]
From the days of King Aelfwald, fornications, adulteries and incest have poured over the land … Consider the way of trimming the beard and hair, the luxurious habits of the princes and the people …

Part of a letter written by the Northumbrian scholar, Alcuin, to Ethelred, King of Northumbria, in 793, after the beginning of the Viking raids.

● **SOURCE 7**

Photograph of the Lindisfarne stone, showing carvings of Viking warriors.

● **SOURCE 8**

The Vikings are doing what they seem to do best: not simply trading but adopting a wide variety of cultural influences from the areas with which they were in contact. This image of the Vikings as easy-going travellers, keen to adopt new traditions and styles, is not one we may be used to and, yet, adaptability has always been one of their strengths.

An archaeologist, Julian Richards, on the Vikings who settled in the Danelaw.

● **SOURCE 9**

An oval brooch found in the grave of a Viking woman at Santon Downham, Norfolk.

● **SOURCE 11**

www.bbc.co.uk/history/ancient/vikings
Standard BBC site: sound and well worth a visit.

www.vikingworld.dk/jellinge48.htm
A site focusing on the Vikings in Denmark but an excellent section on the Vikings in Britain.

www.battle1066.com/vikings2.shtml
Get beyond 1066 when typing this in, otherwise you'll get stuck in the Battle of Hastings! An excellent site.

www.vikingsonline.org.uk
A re-enactment society but a lot of useful information.

There are a lot of websites that can give useful information and ideas about the Vikings. These are some of the most reliable ones. Access them and follow the links.

● **SOURCE 10**

A photograph of some of the chessmen carved by the Vikings and found on the Isle of Lewis in Scotland.

● **SOURCE 12**

It is always a temptation to an armed and agile nation
To call upon a neighbour and to say –
"We invaded you last night – and we are quite prepared to fight,
Unless you pay us cash to go away."

And that is called asking for Dane-geld,
And the people who ask it explain
That you've only to pay 'em the Dane-geld
And then you'll get rid of the Dane!

It is always a temptation to a rich and lazy nation,
To puff and look important and to say –
"Though we know we should defeat you, we have not the time to meet you
We will therefore pay you cash to go away."

And that is called paying the Dane-geld;
But we've proved it again and again,
That if once you have paid him the Dane-geld
You never get rid of the Dane.

In 1911, the poet Rudyard Kipling wrote a poem called 'Danegeld'. These are the first four verses.

● **SOURCE 13**

A model reconstruction of the Battle of Hastings.

● **SOURCE 14**

And there came to meet them [the Danes] prince Edgar and earl Waltheof and Gospatric with the Northumbrians and all the people riding and marching with an immense army rejoicing exceedingly and so they all went resolutely to York and stormed and razed the castle and captured an incalculable treasure in it and killed many hundreds of Frenchmen and took many with them to the ships. When the King [William] found out about this he went northwards with all his army that he could collect, and utterly ravaged and laid waste to that shire.

The *Anglo-Saxon Chronicle*, 1069.

SOURCE 15

King William rode to all the remote parts of his kingdom and fortified strategic sites against enemy attack. For the fortifications called castles by the Normans were scarcely known in the English provinces, and so the English – in spite of their courage and love of fighting – could put up only a weak resistance to their enemies.

Written by Orderic Vitalis (c.1114–51).

SOURCE 16

William, King of the English, to Ethelwig, abbot of Evesham, greeting.
I order you to summon all those who are subject to your administration and jurisdiction that they bring before me at Clarendon at Pentecost all the knights they owe me, duly equipped. You, also, on that day, shall come to me and bring with you fully equipped those five knights which you owe me in respect of your abbacy.

A writ, issued in about 1072, from William to the Abbot of Evesham.

SOURCE 17

We poor wretches destroy the works of our forefathers only to get praise ourselves. The happy age of holy men knew not how to build stately churches: under any roof they offered themselves as living temples to God. But we neglect the care of souls, and labour to heap up stones.

Wulfstan, Bishop of Worcester and the last Saxon bishop left in England, writing in 1095 about the rebuilding of his own cathedral.

SOURCE 18

Verily, William I was a very great prince: full of hope to undertake great enterprises, full of courage to achieve them: in most of his actions commendable, and excusable in all. The kings of England which succeeded him, did count their order only from him. This was not because of his victory in England, but generally in respect of his virtue and valour.

John Hayward, in his book *The Lives of the Three Normans, Kings of England*, from 1613, writing about William I.

SOURCE 19

Alfred's dynasty, which had survived Danes, Norsemen, and Danes again, has succumbed at last to foreign invasion. It was the end of the road for the House of Wessex, but not for Anglo-Saxon society, nor for its institutions and culture. It was essentially by English means that the Norman kings ruled England, and, after the traumatic interlude of conquest, the structures which had made the state so strong between Eadgar and Edward the Confessor reasserted themselves. In a variety of ways, England in 1400 looks startlingly like England in 1000. Hundreds [areas] survived into modern times; shires and sheriffs are still with us; the English language is still spoken. Most fundamentally, it was in the years between 600 and 1100 that English towns, villages and the road-system, and much of the distinctive character of the countryside, took shape.

John Blair in his book *The Anglo-Saxon Age*, published in 1984, writing about the lasting impact of the Saxons into Norman times.

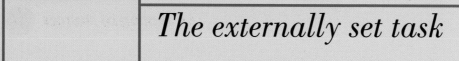

The externally set task

How to succeed with the task

At the end of your course of study of raiders and invaders you will have to complete what the exam board calls an externally set task. You will be given a question and you will have four hours to research, plan and write an answer. These four hours will probably be spread across several of your normal history lessons.

Below is an example of the type of question you will be given.

'Saxons, Vikings and Normans all invaded the British Isles, but only the Saxons were peaceful and civilised; the Vikings and Normans were violent and barbaric.'

How far do the sources you have researched convince you that this statement is correct?

Before you start

From the very start, there are four important things to remember:

1 There is no right answer. What will impress the examiners is how well you support your arguments.
2 The examiner is interested in how well you have answered the question, not in how much you have found out or how much you can write.
3 The question says 'how far do the sources you have researched convince you that this statement is correct?'. This means you need to comment on the sources you have used – have they been useful, do you trust them, do they differ from each other, are there things they do not tell you about? Make sure you have used a wide range of different types of sources: from the medieval period and from later; written sources and illustrations.
4 You must manage your time properly. There is no point in having lots of notes if you don't have time to write your final answer. It would seem sensible to spend roughly two hours on your research, half an hour on sorting everything out and an hour and a half writing up your findings. But this is just a rough guide. A lot depends on how quickly you work and how easy you find the question. But don't worry: a short, well-argued answer that keeps to the question will score more highly than a long, rambling one that contains lots of material but doesn't get to the point.

How to tackle the task

1 Think about what you know already

- How could you decide whether or not people were 'peaceful and civilised' and 'violent and barbaric'? What would you look for? Draw up a checklist.
- Use your notes and other information you have already to see how the Saxons, Vikings and Normans measure up to this checklist.
- Remember that Saxons, Vikings and Normans may have behaved differently at different times.

2 Begin your research

- The task asks you to research sources. You will need to use evidence from a wide range of sources to back up what you are going to say. You could be looking for archaeological evidence, for reconstructions, for what people at the time believed and for what historians think.
- Start with the sources you already have from your work on Part 1 of this book. What does the evidence suggest so far about who comes out best on your checklist?
- Remember to think about the reliability and usefulness of these sources.

3 Wider research

- You can use any resources normally available in your school or college. This means you can use your own books and notes as well as the library and the internet.
- Look for a range of sources that will help you decide what the Saxons, Vikings and Normans were really like. Remember to think about the reliability and usefulness of these sources.
- Keep a note of all the sources you use. You will need to include a list at the end of your answer.
- Look for different opinions about what the Saxons, Vikings and Normans were like. Are these different opinions supported by the evidence you have found?

4 Write up your findings

- Make sure you explain **how far** you agree with the statement given in the question. Do not just write down everything you have found out about the Saxons, Vikings and Normans.
- Try to compare the three groups. If you think one was overall more peaceful and civilised than the others, explain why by comparing them.
- Back up what you say by referring to the sources you have researched.
- Do your best to communicate your findings clearly, and use correct grammar and spelling.

Try the task

You have been given a lot of help with the way in which you should approach the task. This is because the examiners do not want you to spend time figuring out what to do. They are interested in seeing how you do it! Here are some more detailed guidelines that will help you as you work through the four sections of hints for the question on page 48.

1 Think about what you know already

You've probably already decided that there were aspects of Viking and Norman life that were peaceful and civilised just as there were aspects of Saxon life that were very violent and not civilised at all. But don't jump straight in with this. Stand back, and think.

What does it mean to be 'peaceful and civilised'? Here are some ideas: settle quickly; stop trying to get more land; create useful and beautiful objects. What does it mean to be 'violent and barbaric'? Obviously everyone was violent when they were busy raiding and invading, but what about afterwards? Did they overpower the people who were already there or did they try to live peacefully with them? Draw up a checklist of definitions, but don't spend too long on doing this.

It would probably be sensible, now, to draw up a grid that you can use during your research:

	Peaceful and civilised	Violent and barbaric
Saxons		
Vikings		
Normans		

Enter on the grid the sources you research that lead you to believe the Saxons, Vikings and Normans were 'peaceful and civilised' or 'violent and barbaric'. Remember that some sources might lead you to think 'both'. For example, a beautifully engraved dagger handle would imply that only a civilised society would have the skill and the time to produce it – but it was produced to do something violent. So put it in both columns.

2 Begin your research

Begin with the sources in the chapters on Saxons, Vikings and Normans in this book. Don't expect them all to be useful in demonstrating 'peaceful and civilised' or 'violent and barbaric'. You'll need to look back to your checklist of definitions. And don't forget to dip into the ragbag!

By now you will have realised that it isn't enough to sort out the sources: you need to give them a brief context – some sort of explanation as to why they are good examples of 'peaceful and civilised' or 'violent and barbaric'. For example, the archaeological finds in Coppergate, York, could well be used as an example of 'peaceful and civilised' but you'd need to give a brief explanation as to why. For this, you'll need to use the information in this book.

Don't worry if your grid is beginning to swell alarmingly. It might be sensible to have Saxons, Vikings and Normans on separate pages.

3 Wider research

Here you can use your class notes, school or college library and the internet – anything, in fact, that is normally available to you. But before you rush off and start whizzing through microfiches or typing stuff into your favourite search engine, stand back again, and think. What are you going to be looking for?

Go back to your grid. Where are the gaps? Do you have enough material on, for example, the violence of the Saxons or the peaceful nature of the Normans?

Remember, too, to think about the reliability and usefulness of the sources as evidence of 'peaceful and civilised' and 'violent and barbaric'. Then, and only then, when you have a list of gaps, would it be sensible to go looking for material with which to fill them.

Remember to look for different opinions on the Saxons, Vikings and Normans. Where did these come from? How are they backed by the evidence you have found?

4 Write up your findings

Now you need to be really ruthless. Go back to the question. It asks 'How far …' you agree with the statement given in the task. You must **not** write out everything you have researched about the Saxons, Vikings and Normans. Be very selective. Throw out all the sources and information you have collected that looked interesting but are not directly connected with your answer to the question. Keep a note of the sources you have used, including internet sites, in putting your answer together.

Now, as you write up, try to compare the three groups. If you think that, overall, one group was more peaceful and civilised than the others, then say so but remember to back up what you say with hard evidence. As part of this backing up, you will need to say what weight you can give to the evidence you are using – how reliable is it? You may decide that, overall, each group was 'violent and barbaric' and 'peaceful and civilised' but in different ways. In which case, you must say so and, as always, back up what you say with hard evidence you have researched.

Try to write as reasoned and logical an answer as you can. Remember, to get top marks you will need to 'produce well-developed, well-reasoned and well-supported analyses, explanations, arguments and historical conclusions'.

Good luck!

Part 2 Power and control

How to use the material in Part 2

As you have turned to this part of the book it probably means that you are preparing for the GCSE externally set task about medieval monarchs. When you have finished this part of the course you will have to answer a question about medieval monarchs. You will have four hours to research, plan and write your answer. You will be able to use your notes and books and carry out research; however, you will be able to answer the question more easily if you already know and understand quite a lot about medieval monarchs.

The authors of this book do not know the exact question you will be faced with but they do know which monarchs you need to know about and the kind of issues you should be exploring.

You will need to know about three medieval kings of England: John, who was king 1199–1216; Edward I, 1272–1307; and Henry V, 1413–22. You will also need to know about Owain Glyndwr who lived 1359–1416. He rebelled against English rule and claimed the title of Prince of Wales.

The most useful way of finding out about the past is to ask questions about it. Below are some useful questions to ask about each of these rulers. This book helps you to work out your own answers to these questions. Working on these questions will help you answer the task you will be set. You also need to compare the monarchs and ask yourself which rulers were the more successful – and why.

The questions you need to keep asking:

What qualities did a medieval monarch need to be successful?

What were their main achievements and what failures did they have?

How far did each of these three monarchs have these qualities, and what were their strengths and weaknesses?

What impact did they have on the lives of ordinary people: did they make their lives worse or better?

Did they have to deal with similar or different

What methods did they use to make people loyal to them and to control the country?

How can we find out about them and what different views have people had about them – at the time and after they died?

This part of the book is divided into five sections:

Introduction   This will help you understand what medieval monarchs had to do and the difficulties they faced. It will also help you to place them in the right order in the overall history of England.

The kings   This will give you information about the monarchs you have to study as well as asking useful questions about them. It also looks at how these monarchs have been represented in different ways. By the end of this section you should have come to your own judgement about each monarch and be able to compare them.

Owain Glyndwr   This section considers Owain Glyndwr. He was not a king of England but aspired to be Prince of Wales. You need to think about what similarities, and what differences, there were between him and the monarchs.

Summing up   This helps you bring it all together and to compare the monarchs you have been studying.

A practice task   This will take you through how to research, plan and answer the externally set task. It is based on a question like the one you will be set.

Introduction

1 When did these monarchs rule?

It is helpful to have some idea of how these monarchs fit in with the rest of British history. You will have noticed that they are called medieval monarchs. This is because they lived in what we call the Middle Ages.

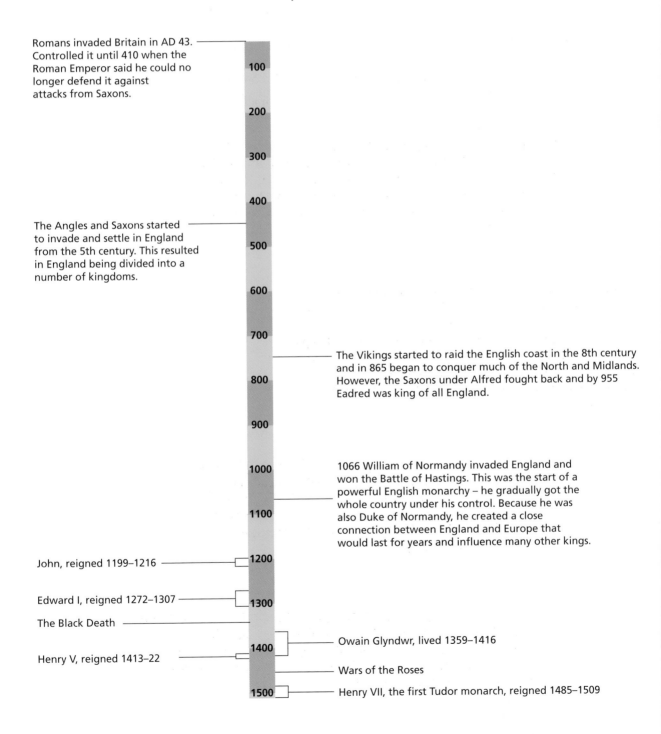

Romans invaded Britain in AD 43. Controlled it until 410 when the Roman Emperor said he could no longer defend it against attacks from Saxons.

The Angles and Saxons started to invade and settle in England from the 5th century. This resulted in England being divided into a number of kingdoms.

The Vikings started to raid the English coast in the 8th century and in 865 began to conquer much of the North and Midlands. However, the Saxons under Alfred fought back and by 955 Eadred was king of all England.

1066 William of Normandy invaded England and won the Battle of Hastings. This was the start of a powerful English monarchy – he gradually got the whole country under his control. Because he was also Duke of Normandy, he created a close connection between England and Europe that would last for years and influence many other kings.

John, reigned 1199–1216

Edward I, reigned 1272–1307

The Black Death

Owain Glyndwr, lived 1359–1416

Henry V, reigned 1413–22

Wars of the Roses

Henry VII, the first Tudor monarch, reigned 1485–1509

Medieval monarchs came in all shapes and sizes. The only thing they had in common was that they were all men. Below you will find some details about the fifteen medieval kings who reigned in the period 1066–1471. You can learn a lot from these details. As you read them make notes about the following questions:

- How many of them had problems becoming king?
- How many of them had problems with members of their family?
- What kinds of things made life dangerous for a new king?
- Which countries did these kings most often fight against?
- How many died natural deaths, how many were murdered and how many died while fighting?
- Which king do you think was the most successful and which one was the biggest failure?
- What do you think were the two biggest problems medieval kings had to face?
- Owain Glyndwr seems to be different from all the others. In what ways was he different?

William I (known as William the Conqueror) lived 1027–87 (reigned 1066–87). Became King of England after defeating King Harold in the Battle of Hastings, 1066. Fought many wars, put down rebellions, defeated an attempted invasion. He died in France, while fighting the French, from injuries sustained when his horse stumbled.

William II (called William Rufus because of his ruddy complexion) 1056–1100 (reigned 1087–1100). Third son of William I. Left the throne by his father and arrived in England before his brother could claim the throne. Had to put down a rebellion by the barons in 1088 and another one later in his reign. Fought against Scotland and Wales as well as France. Shot by an arrow while hunting in England (could have been an accident or murder).

Henry I 1068–1135 (reigned 1100–35). Youngest son of William I. Moved quickly on his brother's death and claimed the throne. Defeated rebellion and invasion by Robert, his elder brother. Fought with France, invaded Wales. He died, while in Normandy, of a gastric attack after eating lampreys.

Stephen 1097–1154 (reigned 1135–54). Son of William I's daughter. Seized the throne when it had been promised to Matilda (daughter of Henry I). She, with support of some of the barons, invaded England and there were civil wars for next 17 years. It was agreed that Matilda's son would become next king. Stephen died in Dover from a heart attack.

Henry II 1133–89 (reigned 1154–89). Son of Matilda, succession not disputed. Put down rebellion in England, had success against Ireland and Scotland, fought in France against his wife and sons. Said to have died from a broken heart in France when he learned that John, his youngest son, had been fighting against him.

Richard I 1157–99 (reigned 1189–99). Oldest surviving son of Henry II. Fought against his father. Forced his father to make him his successor (Henry favoured his younger son John). Spent only six months in England while king. The rest of the time was spent fighting a crusade in the Holy Land or fighting in France. Killed by a bolt from a crossbow while fighting in France.

John 1167–1216 (reigned 1199–1216). Youngest son of Henry II. Defeated in France and lost Normandy. Lost the crown jewels when his baggage train sank in the marshes of the Wash. This affected his health and he died shortly after from fever and diarrhoea – either caused by eating far too much or by poisoning. Was in the middle of a civil war with the barons when he died.

Henry III 1207–72 (reigned 1216–72). Eldest son of John and only nine years old when he became king. Barons supported his succession to prevent the French king taking the English throne. Until 1227, while he was a minor, the country was governed by regents. Attempts by Henry to reassert royal control led to civil war with the barons. Was their prisoner for a time but eventually defeated them. Died naturally.

Edward I 1239–1307 (reigned 1272–1307). Eldest son of Henry. Went on crusade in the Holy Land, conquered Wales, defeated the Scots, and fought in France. Died naturally while on his way to fight a rebellion by the Scots.

Edward II 1284–1327 (reigned 1307–27). Eldest son of Edward I. Fought civil war with the barons. Defeated in battles against the Scots. Defeated in civil war by his wife and forced to give up the throne. Imprisoned and murdered with a red-hot poker.

Edward III 1312–77 (reigned 1327–77). Eldest son of Edward II. His mother governed until 1330 when he seized power and imprisoned her. Fought successful wars against the Scots. By claiming the French throne started the Hundred Years War. Several victories in France and extended English territory there. Had thirteen sons, of whom five lived to maturity (this would cause problems in later years). Died of a heart attack in England.

Richard II 1367–1400 (reigned 1377–99). Eldest son of the Black Prince (Edward III's eldest son) who died one year before his own father. Only ten years old when he became king so his uncle, John of Gaunt, ruled for first few years. Had to deal with the Peasants' Revolt. Defeated by barons in civil war and his power was restricted. He was unpopular with the barons because he did not like fighting wars – indecisive war with Scotland and made peace with France. Led an expedition to Ireland. While he was away, Henry Bolingbroke (John of Gaunt's son), landed in England to claim the throne. Richard was captured and forced to give up the throne. He was either murdered or starved to death. He had no children.

Henry IV 1367–1413 (reigned 1399–1413). Seized the throne from Richard II. Managed to defeat rebellions by Owain Glyndwr of Wales and Henry Percy because of his eldest son Henry's military abilities. Ill for much of his reign from a skin disease and from violent attacks that may have been epilepsy. Died from such an attack. However, his son Henry had really been ruling the country since 1410.

Henry V 1387–1422 (reigned 1413–22). Eldest son of Henry IV. Helped his father to defeat Owain Glyndwr of Wales, and invaded Scotland. Spent most of his reign fighting in France for the French crown. Defeated the French at Agincourt and on other occasions. Died in France while on a military campaign.

Henry VI 1421–71 (reigned 1422–71). Only son of Henry V. Only one year old when became king. During his minority the country was governed by a council. Nearly all lands in France were lost. During Henry's mental breakdown, Richard, Duke of York (descended from Edward III) was appointed protector. When Henry recovered, Richard fought him to keep his power – the beginning of the Wars of the Roses. Henry lost the throne, then regained it, before being murdered.

Owain Glyndwr 1359–1416. Claimed he was descended from Llewelyn, the last Prince of Wales who died in 1240. Owned estates in Wales. Fought for Richard II against the Scots but when Henry IV came to the throne he headed the Welsh rebellion and took the title 'Prince of Wales'. Appealed for support from Scotland and Ireland. Allied with France. Had victories against England but also defeats. Still fighting when he died around 1416.

2 A few things you need to know

(You might have worked some of these out for yourself as you were doing the previous exercise.)

How did someone become king?

William had taken the throne by force by defeating Harold at the Battle of Hastings. For some time after him, becoming king was what one historian has described as smash-and-grab. As you have seen, William's eldest son Robert never got the throne because first his younger brother William, and then his other younger brother Henry both grabbed the throne before he could. Sometimes the dying wishes of the old king were followed but not always.

However, as we get further into the Middle Ages, the idea that the eldest son should succeed to the throne on his father's death became more accepted. This was connected to another idea, that kings were chosen by God. God had set them up above everyone else to protect and govern. Everybody had a duty to obey the king. Kings were very keen on this idea because it meant that to oppose them was to go against God. However, the idea also said that kings had to govern well, for the good of everybody. This might cause problems for some kings. They were after all only human; some of them made mistakes and some were simply bad or weak kings. This led to the question – did the nobles have the right to rebel against a king if he did not provide good government?

Kings and their nobles

William and the Norman kings who followed him, obsessed with war and power as they were, made the monarchy stronger. As the monarchy's power grew the nobles became more determined to limit its powers. They wanted a strong king but they did not want the king to be all-powerful, and they certainly wanted him to obey the law as everybody else did. They also wanted to have a say in the government of the country. They thought they had a right and a duty to help the king govern the country.

It became common for the king to hold a Great Council made up of barons, bishops and his most important officials, to ask their advice, gather information and issue instructions.

There was no way that a king could govern the country by himself. Remember the nobles were rich and powerful with their own soldiers. They basically ran their parts of the country on behalf of the king. He also depended on them when he needed an army and he needed them to keep large parts of the country under control and to dispense justice. In return they wanted a say in the big decisions! As some kings discovered to their cost, if they lost the support of the barons they were in trouble!

● **SOURCE A**

Lands held by Henry II.

Key

■ Lands held by Henry II as King

▨ Lands held from the King of France

▦ Lands held by marriage

▨ Lands claimed by Henry but controlled by others

Were the English kings really English?

When you were completing the exercise on medieval monarchs (page 55), you were probably surprised by the fact that some of the kings seemed more interested in Europe than they were in England. There were very good reasons for this – they were not really English and they also controlled large amounts of territory in Europe. Remember that William the Conqueror had come from Europe where he was Duke of Normandy. The kings that followed him inherited land in Europe as well as England. This land had to be defended, especially from the French king. It is also important to remember that several of the kings were born or brought up in Europe. Their first language was French!

This European dimension of the English monarchy became even more important when Henry II became king in 1154. He was the first Angevin king (this means he was son of Geoffrey, the Count of Anjou). Henry was French and inherited a vast European empire that stretched to Spain, as well as Normandy and England. Many of the English medieval kings spent much of their time defending and even expanding these lands in Europe. Some of them spent more time out of England than in and regarded the lands in Europe as the heart of their empire.

The importance of the Church and going on a crusade

Medieval kings had inside their country one organisation over which they did not have control – the Roman Catholic Church which was led by the Pope in Rome.

It was very powerful because it was the only organisation that was represented in just about every village in the land. There you would find a church and a priest. Another reason for its power was that everybody believed in God, and in heaven and hell. Everybody went to church every week and they all depended on the priest for getting to heaven after they died. For these reasons medieval kings were constantly trying to gain more power over the Church.

It was regarded as the duty of a Christian king to go on a crusade to help win back Jerusalem and the Holy Land from Muslims. Richard I, known as the Lionheart, is the English king most closely associated with the crusades. He spent most of his reign on one. His brother King John did not go on a crusade, but Edward I did. By the time Henry V was king crusades had long faded away.

Wales, Scotland and Ireland

You probably noticed from the exercise on medieval monarchs that many of them spent a lot of time fighting in Wales, Scotland and Ireland. No English king could feel totally secure until he had control over these countries. When William I became king, Wales was a collection of small kingdoms and it was not always clear where Wales stopped and England started. The Welsh were racially different from the English and had their own language. The Normans conquered some parts of Wales but the real conquest of Wales did not happen until Edward I's reign at the end of the thirteenth century.

Scotland was poorer and the English kings had less reason to want to conquer it. Scotland was also harder to conquer as it was larger and was a unified kingdom. Edward I conquered Scotland for a time but this was not permanent and Scotland regained its independence. Ireland was only partly conquered. The area of English rule was called the 'pale' and outside this was Gaelic-speaking Ireland with its own Irish kings.

How kings affected ordinary people

Medieval kings did not affect the lives of ordinary people in the direct way that governments do today. They did not provide hospitals, schools and pensions. Most people spent their days toiling on the land and rarely left the village they were born in. News from London could take weeks to filter down into local areas. For most peasants the lord of the manor was a far more important figure than the king. However, there were two ways in which the king might affect their lives. Firstly, he had a responsibility to provide peace, stability and law and order so that people could live their lives without fear of violence. A weak king whose reign descended into civil war would bring disorder and lawlessness into the lives of ordinary people. Secondly, the king could cause hardship by taxing people too harshly and seizing supplies for his armies. However, we must remember that kings had no control over the major things that affected people's lives – the weather, disease and poor harvests.

3 What made a good medieval king?

Being a medieval king was a difficult job. Medieval kings were very different from modern kings and queens because they had power – lots of it. A king in the Middle Ages owned enormous amounts of land, was very rich and governed the country (with help from his advisers). But if he did not do a good job, he might be overthrown by the nobles. Also, there was always the threat of being attacked by other countries.

A king had to:

rule the country for the good of everybody, and not just for his own good

have a strong claim to the throne that people would recognise

spend money wisely and not tax the people too heavily

have leadership qualities so that people would respect, follow and obey him

make sure that the justice system worked properly and that people were treated fairly by the law

get on well with the nobles and choose advisers they would approve of (he could not govern the country without the help of the nobles). Some of these nobles would be related to him and might be after the throne themselves

keep law and order across the country so people could lead their lives in peace

lead his armies to defend the country and to win new lands – the nobles expected this

keep on good terms with the Church (which was very powerful)

have healthy sons (to be his heirs) to make sure there would not be a civil war over who would succeed him

Task

Look at the list of qualities below. Choose the three most important ones for a medieval king. Explain how the three you have chosen would help him do the job well. Add to the list two other qualities that you think were important.

honest   religious   greedy   healthy   respected   clever

ruthless   fair   handsome   cruel   brave   musical

funny   feared   hated   lazy   educated

4 Three young princes: who would you put your money on?

This section considers how well prepared our three kings were when they became king. Did they have a good claim to the throne? Did they have the right personal qualities? Did they have the right kind of experience? The information about each one is presented in the form of a CV, as if they were applying for the job of king. You have to decide which one you think had the best chance of being a good king. The chart below will help you to organise your thoughts about this. Copy the chart and then complete it – score each of the three princes on a scale 1–5 (1 is bad, 5 is good) in each of the four categories. You need to give some supporting evidence each time to explain the score you have given.

	Strong claim to the throne?	Right personal qualities?	Relevant experience?	Successes or failures so far?	Total
Prince John					
Prince Edward					
Prince Henry					

Prince John

Personal details

Became king when he was 32 years old and his elder brother Richard died without any children. There was someone else who had a claim to the throne – Arthur the son of John's elder brother Geoffrey. Arthur was only a boy and John had him murdered.

Character/personality

Unfortunately, his barons, and historians, often compared him with his elder brother Richard the Lionheart who is shown as nearly superhuman – a great Crusader and a warrior of strength and skill. John did not look good in comparison.

John had a bad temper and violent rages that left him foaming at the mouth. Here is a description

by an eyewitness of John when he was a prince: 'His whole person became so changed as to be hardly recognisable. Rage contorted his brow, his burning eyes glittered, bluish spots discoloured the pink of his cheeks.' He is often described as scheming and cowardly. One historian has described him as 'shifty, greedy, cruel, vindictive and self-serving'. Another has said 'John was always without nobility and honesty'.

John plotted with Richard against their father Henry II. When Henry learned about John's treachery he died two days later, apparently from heartbreak. After becoming king, Richard wanted to ban John from England while he was away on crusade because he did not trust him. However, their mother persuaded him to change his mind but, while Richard was away, John plotted behind his back for the throne. While he was on his way home to deal with his brother, Richard was taken prisoner. John used the opportunity to plot with the king of France. John declared Richard dead and himself king. He even tried to stop Richard being released. When Richard returned he quickly defeated the rebels. John flung himself to the floor in front of Richard in tears; Richard picked him up and said 'Think no more of it John, you are only a child' (he was 27 at the time).

Experience

An unfortunate childhood. He was bullied and saw his mother and elder brothers spending most of their time scheming and rebelling against his father. This may have made him shifty and untrustworthy.

John was Henry's fourth son so he never expected to be king. For a long time he does not seem to have figured in his father's plans at all. Even when Henry died he left John no land (hence John's nickname 'Lackland'). He was often ridiculed by his father and ignored by his mother (who doted on Richard). This made him very insecure. He grew up trusting no one and thinking everyone was plotting behind his back. He only became king because his two eldest brothers died young, and the next brother Richard died without children.

All this meant that he was not given much responsibility. However, in 1185 when he was eighteen, John was sent over to Ireland with a small army to sort out some problems. He was a disaster, managing to upset everyone. He was called home after six months.

Prince Edward

Personal details

Eldest son of Henry III; no rivals for the throne. Edward was 33 years old when he became king. He was physically impressive: 6 feet 2 inches tall, which gave him the nickname 'Longshanks'. First of the medieval kings to speak English as his first language and was named after the great Anglo-Saxon king Edward the Confessor, who had been made a saint.

Character/personality

Addicted to jousting and took any challenge to his bravery and strength very seriously. Edward was liable to outbursts of uncontrolled temper – when a youth got in his way by accident he ordered him to be savagely mutilated.

When Edward learned that he had become king he was in Sicily on his way back from a crusade. While on crusade he was stabbed in an attempt to murder him by a poisoned dagger. He fought off the assassin with a stool and snatched the dagger from him. The poison had to be sucked from the wound and surgeons made a mess of his arm.

Edward was ruthless and had a vicious cruel streak. After he defeated Simon de Montfort in battle he had his hands, feet and testicles cut off. His genitals were hung around his nose. Some of Simon's wounded soldiers were killed as they lay helpless. He also hunted down Simon's relatives one by one. A poem written in the 1260s compared him to a lion and a leopard (lions were admired as brave and strong but leopards were devious – clever but not to be trusted).

Edward was deeply in love with his wife Eleanor who bore him fifteen children. They were married for 36 years and Edward fell apart when she died. He had Eleanor crosses built at each place where her funeral procession stopped on its journey from Lincoln to London.

Experience

His father's reign had been a very difficult one. Henry III had been only nine when he became king and so the country had to be governed by barons. When Henry was old enough he tried to reassert royal control. But the barons, led by Simon de Montfort, demanded the right to have a say over who the king chose as his advisers. They also wanted to shift power from the king to a Parliament of barons. This resulted in civil war in the 1260s. Without Edward, Henry would have lost the civil war. It was Edward who won over some of the barons to his side, and it was Edward who led the royal armies and defeated the barons. Edward saved the monarchy.

Edward began to take a part in public affairs from the age of twelve. He was made Duke of Gascony by his father, and was soon popular there. In 1256 the merchants in Gascony complained they were being extorted by royal officials. Edward got this stopped. However, he did not do so well in Wales where he introduced high taxes and forced the Welsh into a rebellion that went on for eleven years.

Here is a historian's conclusion about Edward: 'By the time he was crowned in 1274 Edward had seen pretty much everything that medieval politics and warfare could put a prince's way.'

Prince Henry

Personal details

Henry was 26 years old when he became king. He was Henry IV's eldest son. However, his father had taken the throne from Richard II. Not everyone had accepted Henry IV as king and he had to put down several rebellions. There was unrest for the remaining years of his reign and when Henry V became king there were still doubts about his right to the throne. There were some nobles who wanted his younger brother, the Duke of Clarence, to become the new king. Luckily for Henry, his brother was in France when their father died. Henry IV left his son a government heavily in debt and the country plagued by disorder.

Character/personality

By the time he became king Henry V had already developed a reputation as being a brave conquering hero, a charismatic warrior who won the loyalty of those who fought with him. At the Battle of Shrewsbury he was wounded by an arrow in the face but insisted on fighting on. He is seen as arrogant and determined, but also very religious. Some accounts say that as a youth he was a wild tearaway, frequenting taverns and being involved in drunken brawls. He was ambitious – on one occasion his father got very angry when he found Henry trying on the crown.

One historian has said 'By the time of his accession to the throne in 1413, Henry was a man who knew how to lead others and who expected to be obeyed.'

Experience

As Henry IV's eldest son he was made Prince of Wales. He was only fourteen when Owain Glyndwr declared himself as Prince of Wales and started a Welsh rebellion against English rule. By 1402 Henry was in charge of operations against the Welsh. He took a leading role in defeating the Percys in 1403 in the Battle of Shrewsbury and by 1406 he was well on the way to defeating the Welsh.

As his father's health declined Henry became more powerful. From 1406 he attended the King's Council and by 1410 he was running the country. However, his father's health returned and relations between them became strained for the rest of the reign.

5 Shaping our views

You might think that our views of these three kings are simply based on what they did and how successful they were. Of course, what they did is an important factor but our view about anyone in the past is also influenced by other factors.

Firstly, we depend on what people at the time wrote down about the kings. They might give us a biased view like the monks writing about John (see Sources A and B on the facing page).

Secondly, whether a king was successful or not is not necessarily a point of fact; it is an opinion. This means that there is plenty of opportunity for people to disagree. All you can do is look at the evidence carefully and make up your own mind.

Thirdly, the views we have today about these kings are not just influenced by what the kings did. They are also influenced by what has been said, written and drawn about them. For example, when Britain has been fighting a war Henry V has often been used as an example of a great war leader.

Each of our three kings has his own popular image. We are going to investigate how these have been created over the years. If you were to ask someone today about these kings, or if they are mentioned on the TV, or in a magazine, this is what is normally said about each of them:

John: a bad, cruel and cowardly king who was a disaster. He lost English lands in France and was forced by the barons to sign the Magna Carta which lost the monarchy much of its power.

Nicknames – Lackland, Softsword.

Edward: a strong king who brought law and order after the anarchy of his father's reign and conquered the Welsh (building lots of castles there) and defeated the Scots.

Nicknames – Hammer of the Scots, Longshanks (he was 1.85m – very tall for those days).

Henry: a heroic king who reformed from being a wild youth to a great warrior king who won the Battle of Agincourt against all the odds.

No nicknames.

Discussion point

What do their nicknames or lack of nicknames tell us about them?

You are now going to explore how and why these views of these three kings have been created.

The making of bad King John

A monk from St Alban's Abbey wrote an account of John's reign ten years after he died. Here are some of the things he wrote about John:

● **SOURCE A**

In 1209 he had a clergyman crushed under a cope [stone] of lead and he died an agonising death.

He ordered that a Jew should have a tooth knocked out daily until he revealed where his treasure was hidden.

John let people go who had robbed and murdered priests.

Roger of Wendover.

Should we trust what Roger wrote about John?

* He claimed to know John's exact words when he spoke to people – is this likely?
* Some of the stories he told were very odd, for example, an old woman who worked on a Sunday was sucked dry by a small black pig as a punishment – does this mean his other stories about John are reliable?
* Government documents show that the clergyman who was meant to be crushed under a cope of lead in 1209 was still alive in 1225 and had become a bishop!
* Roger of Wendover was not a historian. He said he was writing to show people that 'examples of evil men are not to be followed'.
* Government documents show that John ordered that anyone harming a clergyman should be hanged from an oak tree.
* John had several quarrels with the Church and the Pope even excommunicated him (threw him out of the Church).

Another monk who was at St Alban's Abbey just after Roger got hold of Roger's account and spiced it up in places. This is how he described John.

● **SOURCE B**

John was a tyrant not a king, a destroyer instead of a governor, crushing his own people. He had lost the duchy of Normandy and many other lands because of his laziness. He invaded and destroyed his subjects' property. He gave orders that his wife's lovers were to be seized and strangled on her bed. He seduced the more attractive daughters and sisters of the barons.

Matthew Paris.

When historians in Victorian times came to write history books about John they depended on what monks like Roger and Matthew said. One of the most popular history books ever written was J R Green's *Short History of the English People* written in the 1880s. Green said that even hell was made a worse place when John arrived there! Here is a passage from Green's book. Can you see how he has been influenced by the monks?

● **SOURCE C**

In his inner soul John was the worst outcome of the Angevins. His punishments were refinements of cruelty, the starvation of children, the crushing of old men under copes of lead. His court was a brothel where no woman was safe from the royal lust. He was superstitious but scoffed at priests. He turned his back on the mass even during his coronation, but he never went on a journey without relics round his neck.

J R Green, *Short History of the English People*, 1880s.

This became the popular view of John. You can see from the next extract written in a children's encyclopaedia in the 1930s that views of John had not changed.

● **SOURCE D**

A cold-hearted, selfish man sat alone in a quiet room in a palace, and his thoughts were cunning and bad. It was John, the king who, by his weakness and foolishness, would unite the whole nation against him.

His cruelty and selfishness lost him the support of the whole nation. His cowardice in the affair with the Pope disgusted them. He tried to bully his nobles, but in this too he failed.

Newnes Pictorial Knowledge, 1930s.

The popular view of bad King John has not changed even to this day. The popularity of the Robin Hood stories has helped in this. These stories tell of an evil John destroying people's freedoms. Although some historians have questioned this view of John they have been powerless against popular films like Walt Disney's *Robin Hood*. These stories have also created a clear contrast between his brother Richard I – who is seen as saintly and perfect (despite only spending one year of his reign in England), brave and honest – and poor old John who is shifty, greedy and cruel.

● **SOURCE E**

This is how John appears in the Disney film *Robin Hood*.

Task

Look at Sources B, C and D. Find ten words that they have used to make John seem bad.

How Edward became the hard man

If asked what they know about Edward I most people will come up with two things: castles, and his nickname 'Hammer of the Scots'.

Edward built massive castles all over Wales to keep it under his control. Look at this photograph of Harlech Castle:

● **SOURCE F**

Harlech Castle.

Task

Edward's popular image is shaped by these castles. In the following list of words and phrases are six that historians have used to describe Edward and which are clearly influenced by the castles he built. Which six are they? Explain the reasons for your choice.

clever, coarse, determined, generous, granite-hard, happy, kind, stern, repressive, ruthless, single-minded, sympathetic, thick-skinned, weak.

The popular impression of Edward has also been influenced by the words that were engraved on his tombstone: 'Here lies Edward I, Hammer of the Scots'. These words reinforce ideas of strength and ruthlessness.

Edward's reputation has also been shaped in recent years by the 1995 Hollywood blockbuster *Braveheart*. This film painted a romantic picture of William Wallace leading the Scots in a fight for their freedom from English oppression. It won five Oscars and was an enormous commercial success. Mel Gibson played William Wallace as brave, charismatic and heroic. On the other hand Edward I was shown as 'creepily ruthless'. Can you think of any reasons why the film did this? Here are two possibilities: cinema audiences like to support the underdog; and at the time the film was made there were several small countries fighting for their independence.

Discussion point

Look at these two stills from the film. How do these two representations give different impressions of Edward and William Wallace?

● **SOURCE G**

Patrick McGoohan as Edward I in the film *Braveheart.*

● **SOURCE H**

Mel Gibson as William Wallace in the film *Braveheart.*

Henry V: creating a hero

The popular view of Henry V as a great king has been largely created by William Shakespeare in his play *Henry V*. For much of his information about Henry, Shakespeare used the work of a historian called Holinshed who published a history of England in 1578. This is what he wrote about Henry.

● **SOURCE I**

This Henry was a king, of life without blemish, a prince whom all men loved, and none hated, a captain against whom fortune never frowned, nor bad luck once spurned, whose people both loved and obeyed him. He left no offence unpunished, no friendship unrewarded, he was a terror to rebels, his virtues were famous and his qualities most praiseworthy.

Holinshed, *History of England,* 1578.

Today, most people know Henry V from the speech that Shakespeare gave Henry on the eve of the Battle of Agincourt on 25 October: St Crispin's Day, 1415. Henry's army was cut off from escape, many of them had fallen ill, and they were faced with a much larger French army. In Shakespeare's play Henry shows great leadership qualities. He rallies his troops, lifts their spirits and restores their morale by making this speech. Get your teacher to read it out to you in class or watch a clip of a film of the play. Our idea of what Henry V was like has been completely moulded by the speech. And yet the speech was made up by Shakespeare. Henry never actually said these words!

Discussion point

What different ways has Shakespeare used to get across Henry's qualities?

● **SOURCE J**

He that shall live this day, and see old age,
Will yearly on the vigil feast his neighbours,
And say 'To-morrow is Saint Crispian.'
Then will he strip his sleeve and show his scars,
And say 'These wounds I had on Crispin's day.'
Old men forget; yet all shall be forgot,
But he'll remember, with advantages,
What feats he did that day: then shall our names,
Familiar in his mouth as household words
Harry the King, Bedford and Exeter,
Warwick and Talbot, Salisbury and Gloucester,
Be in their flowing cups freshly remember'd.
This story shall the good man teach his son;
And Crispin Crispian shall ne'er go by,
From this day to the ending of the world,
But we in it shall be remember'd;
We few, we happy few, we band of brothers;
For he to-day that sheds his blood with me
Shall be my brother; be he ne'er so vile,
This day shall gentle his condition;
And gentlemen in England now a-bed
Shall think themselves accurs'd they were not here,
And hold their manhoods cheap whiles any speaks
That fought with us upon St Crispin's day.

William Shakespeare, *Henry V*, 1599.

● **SOURCE K**

A still from a film version of Shakespeare's *Henry V*. It shows the actor Laurence Olivier as Henry.

Task

1 Using Sources I, J and K, write down ten words that sum up what Henry V was like.

2 You now know something about popular ideas about these three kings. Write down the three words for each king that best sum up what they appear to be like. When you have done that check out a couple of the websites mentioned below and see if they give similar impressions of these kings.

www.bbc.co.uk/history
www.britannia.com/history/monarchs
www.spartacus.schoolnet.co.uk

This is what one historian has written about King John.

● SOURCE 1

The character of this tough rather stout, energetic little man [he was about 1.65 metres tall] *defies description because he had so many different moods. He was cruel and ruthless, violent and passionate, greedy and self-indulgent, genial and repellent, clever and capable. He is made up of inconsistencies.*

Austin Lane Poole, 1951.

There is no question that John's reign ended in disaster – he had lost most of his lands in France, there was a civil war, the country had been invaded by the French, and he had no money left! Some have claimed that John failed not because he was necessarily a bad ruler but because he was a poor politician, meaning that he did not know how to get on with the people that mattered – the barons. They simply ended up not trusting him. See if you agree with this point of view.

Losing an empire

John's inheritance

As you can see from the map on page 59 John inherited vast lands in France. Remember, as far as people at the time were concerned John was not an English king with some lands in France, he was a European ruler with a European empire. The heart of this empire was as much in France as it was in England. In his coronation ceremony his first oath had been to protect these lands. However, there were problems: Philip, the French king, was keen to expand France and the areas held by England were obvious targets; John had been left no money by Richard; and Brittany declared its support to Arthur, John's rival for the throne. Some historians have argued that for John to hold on to his lands in Europe was almost an impossible task.

A good soldier?

John has a reputation of being a coward and a poor military leader – hence his nickname 'Softsword'. However, this reputation is partly unfair. In the early years of his reign John led his armies with skill and a good sense of strategy. After building up powerful alliances, a successful war ended with a treaty in 1200 where John's lands in France were recognised. John had achieved this by making a daring dash south into Brittany. This was a masterstroke and caught Philip by surprise. However, it was making peace with France in 1200 that caused John to be given the popular nickname of 'Softsword'. Many thought that he should have gone on from a position of strength and won more victories. When war broke out again in 1202 things did not go so well for John. But he also had victories in Scotland, Ireland and Wales. Interestingly, John never lost a battle in which he was personally leading the army.

The murder of Arthur

When Richard I died without children there were two people who had a claim to the throne: John (Richard's only surviving brother), and twelve-year-old Arthur (son of John's elder brother). When John was given the throne, Arthur allied with the king of France against John. In 1202 John captured Arthur and a number of French barons. His cruel treatment of them made him very unpopular: 22 of the captives were starved to death, Arthur's sister Eleanor was imprisoned for forty years and Arthur disappeared, probably murdered. One account from the time tells of a drunken John killing Arthur with his own hands in a rage and throwing the body into the River Seine. John had been doing well in the war with France but this action helped turn victory into defeat. His enemies hated him even more, his allies deserted him, and even his own barons lost interest in fighting for him.

Disaster in France!

You have seen how the murder of Arthur lost John a lot of support. As John's allies and barons deserted him John's empire began to crumble. By 1206, John had lost Normandy, Brittany, Anjou and Maine. Only Aquitaine remained. It was a disaster. The recovery of these lands remained one of John's aims for the rest of his reign. Preparations were made to win back Normandy in 1205. A massive fleet was assembled but the barons refused to support John. He then showed his complete lack of understanding of how to win the loyalty of his barons by accusing one of them of treason. The accused baron said to the others, 'Let this be a warning to you: what the king is planning to do to me, he will do to every one of you when he gets the upper hand.' The other barons backed away from John who made things worse by screaming, 'By God's teeth, it is plain to see that none of my barons are with me in this: it looks ugly, I must take counsel with my bachelors.' This referred to the young men who John was taking advice from instead of his barons.

John's last expedition was in 1214. While he successfully led his army in Aquitaine, disaster struck his army in Normandy. It was smashed by the French at the Battle of Bouvines. The lands that had been lost in the early years of the reign were now lost for good. He still had Aquitaine but that was all. John's failure cast a shadow over the rest of his reign. The barons lost any feeling of loyalty they may have had towards him and began to sense the stink of defeat surrounding the king. It was no coincidence that after the Battle of Bouvines there was a rebellion in the north of England and in 1215, just one year later, the barons were forcing Magna Carta on the king.

Discussion point

How far was it John's fault that he lost his lands in France?

Good government?

You have seen how John did in Europe. But what about England? Did he govern the country well?

Justice

As you know, one of the first duties of a king was to provide justice and good government for his subjects. How far did John succeed in doing this?

John was determined to govern personally. One historian has said about this: 'It required unbounded energy and universal competence. John had it.' While he was in England, John spent most of his time on the move, up and down the country, making sure that it was being governed properly. As he travelled he personally heard many important court cases and consulted with sheriffs about local issues. The popular image of John as lazy seems to be completely wrong and due entirely to Roger of Wendover's account of him.

John was capable of compassion as is shown by the case he heard of a boy who had thrown a stone and accidentally killed another: John granted a pardon. There is much evidence from the time of people respecting John's wisdom and asking for him to hear their case. John had a firm hand on the system and also seems to have been wise in choosing capable officials to work in his government.

But what about taxes?

John had the bad luck of being king at a time of high inflation and when government was having to take on much more work than ever before. This cost a lot of money. Kings were meant to live off the money from their lands but, as government took on wider responsibilities, this became harder to manage. The solution was for the king to levy taxes and for this he needed the barons' consent. There was some opposition to the tax John levied in 1207 and that was the last time the barons agreed to one. This meant that he had to squeeze every other way he had of raising money like increasing the fines people paid in court and fining every small infringement of the forest laws. One chronicler wrote: 'King John was a pillager of his subjects and this is why they did not support him and little mourned his death.'

Upsetting the barons

John also made as much money as he could from his feudal rights. For example, when a baron succeeded to his father's estates he had to pay the king a fee. The king could charge what he liked and John started to charge more and more. He also forced the widows of barons to marry again because he could charge them a fee for this. Many people at the time saw John's government as grasping and money-grubbing. However, the barons were partly to blame because they refused to accept that the king could no longer run the country from his normal sources of income. They eventually rebelled (see next page).

Upsetting the Pope

It was not very clever of John to pick a fight with Pope Innocent III in 1208 soon after he had lost many of his lands in Europe. John refused to accept the Pope's choice for Archbishop of Canterbury. The Pope responded by placing England under an interdict. This meant that there could be no Christian burials,

marriages or masses in England. You would think this was a disaster for most people and yet there appears to have been little popular unrest. In 1209 John was excommunicated, which means he was thrown out of the Church. Neither John nor his barons seem to have been too bothered about this. But in 1213 John backed down and even handed over the country to the Pope! Some historians see this as a humiliating surrender, while others see it as a clever move. John solved one of his problems, and now had the Pope as his overlord, which meant in practice he would have the Pope as a powerful supporter.

Case study: Was Magna Carta a failure?

In 1215 the barons rose up in rebellion against John because he had failed in his political skills. He had failed to work with the barons, and had failed to win their support and loyalty. Peace in England depended on the king and the barons working together. Of course, there had always been quarrels between king and barons and there had been rebellions in several of the reigns before John's. So why did this rebellion end in Magna Carta?

The King treated us badly.

John, like all medieval kings, had power over a wide range of things – jobs, titles, the right to marry, the right to succeed to land. Like all kings, John sold these to the nobles to make money for himself. But John went to extremes. He charged huge amounts of money and drove several landowners into debt and exile. John also used this power to force men to be loyal to him. John was hopeless at inspiring loyalty in his barons and so he used these other methods to try to get the barons to support him. He failed and instead caused enormous resentment among the barons. One historian has called the civil war that broke out 'a rebellion of the King's debtors'.

In 1213 John de Lacy agreed to pay John £4,666 to succeed to his father's estates. He was promised that if he was loyal to the king this amount would be reduced. He stayed loyal to John until 1215 when he was pardoned all his debts. As soon as this happened he joined the rebels against John.

Why should we support a failed king?

By 1215 John was seen as a total failure. He came to the throne as the ruler of the most powerful state in Europe but within a few years had lost most of his lands. Remember these lands were not outlying parts of an English empire. They were at the heart of an empire of which England was just a part. By losing these lands the empire had been torn apart. John knew he had to get these lands back and spent much of the rest of his reign preparing for this. When he did make an attempt in 1214 his army was totally defeated at the Battle of Bouvines. As soon as John knew of the defeat he began to prepare for civil war. The barons were not going to put up with such humiliation.

We had to find a way of making John behave!

Normally the barons would have tried to replace John as king. However, there were no likely candidates around at the time. They needed something as a rallying cry for their supporters so they came up with the charter. This had to win support and so they made sure it contained something for everyone.

In 1215 they marched on London. By May they had control of all of the capital except the Tower of London. John had no choice but to ask for a truce. In June negotiations took place at Runnymede by the River Thames. Before the end of the month John had agreed to Magna Carta.

Just a charter for the barons?

Magna Carta contains 60 clauses. Here are some of the main ones. You can see that some clauses are obviously aimed at helping the barons but others were designed to win more general support for the barons in their struggle against the king.

Discussion point

Which clauses were for the barons and which were to win general support? Which clause do you think is the most important?

- When a baron inherits land he shall pay the king no more than £100.
- The king is not allowed to make widows remarry against their wishes.
- The guardian of estates belonging to a child should only take reasonable sums of money from the estates.
- The king's men will not take anyone's goods without paying for them.
- Freemen can only be put into prison after being found guilty at a trial with a jury.
- Taxes cannot be levied without the agreement of the bishops and barons.
- The king cannot sell or delay justice to anyone.
- Twenty-five barons were given the job of making sure that John obeyed the Charter.

Historians have disagreed about the importance of Magna Carta. Here are two different ways of looking at it.

1 A great charter of liberty

Magna Carta was the fundamental law of liberty that all our basic freedoms are based on. It stopped kings ruling the country as despots. It established that the law was not just what the king wanted. It was something above the king that he had to obey like everyone else. Its importance is shown by the fact that every time a medieval king tried to rule unfairly the barons would get him to swear to obey Magna Carta. This would remind him that he could not do what he wanted – he had to obey the law of the land. Later in this book you will see the barons doing exactly this with Edward I when he stepped out of line.

In many ways the importance of Magna Carta has grown over the years. The Americans turned to it when they came to write their constitution in the eighteenth century, as the following extract shows: 'Nor shall any persons be deprived of life, liberty or property, without due process of law.'

When a British memorial was set up for the assassinated American President John F Kennedy, to recognise him as a champion of liberty, it was put up at Runnymede!

2 The selfishness of the barons

Magna Carta was a backward-looking document. It was trying to recreate a non-existent golden age when king and barons lived in perfect harmony. It was not a charter of liberty but an attempt to stop the king doing certain things that the barons did not like. If you look at it carefully you can see that much of it is about protecting the barons and stopping the king from getting his hands on their money.

The barons were not trying to bring justice and freedom to everyone. For a start, many of the clauses refer to 'freemen'. This meant that the majority of people, who were not freemen, were left out. And anyway, the barons only included freemen to win their support. All they were really interested in was themselves.

It was a total failure. It was meant to stop the king and barons fighting but John had no intention of obeying it. The creation of a council of 25 barons to make sure John obeyed the Magna Carta meant that John had lost his power as king. There was no way he, or any other king, could put up with this. By the end of 1215 John had rejected Magna Carta and had got the Pope to condemn it as well. He then launched an all-out war. The fighting went on into 1216. By now John was fighting both the barons and the French, who had invaded. The French king was claiming the English throne!

When John died in October 1216 London had fallen to his enemies and he was in a desperate position. In fact his death was probably the best thing that could have happened for the monarchy because the barons then rallied around his nine-year-old son Henry and made him king. No one wanted a French king!

Look at Sources 2 and 3, which are paintings of the signing of Magna Carta. Both were painted *c.* 1900. (Source 3 now hangs in the Houses of Parliament so you can see it if you visit.) Do they give different impressions of the event?

SOURCE 2

SOURCE 3

Making England secure

John knew that England's borders were under threat. The threat in the west and the north came from Ireland, Scotland and Wales. The threat in the south came from France, especially after he had lost his lands in France. John followed a deliberate policy to strengthen the security of England that benefited England for centuries afterwards.

John also showed himself to be a capable leader of an army. A chronicler of the time summed up John's achievements: 'there was now no one in Ireland, Scotland or Wales, who did not bow to his nod, a situation which as is well known, none of his predecessors had achieved.'

Scotland was particularly important because of the troublesome barons in the north of England. If they joined with the Scots there would be real trouble. At the beginning of John's reign William the Lion, King of Scotland, refused to recognise John as his overlord and also claimed the northern counties of England. The situation became more tense in 1209 when some of the northern barons began not only to plot against John, but to plot with Philip of France as well. John marched north with a large army and got what he wanted – William's complete humiliation. William recognised John as his overlord and handed over his two daughters as hostages as a guarantee of his future good behaviour.

Richard I had neglected **Ireland** and let it develop into a bloody free for all. Irish princes and nobles from England grabbed as much land as possible. Royal authority was weak inside the Pale, and hardly existed outside it. In 1210 John led a large army to Ireland. He had a series of excellent victories and asserted his royal power there in a way that had never been achieved before. Although he did not conquer the whole country he had laid the foundations for English power in Ireland.

Wales was also a mess when John became king. The south was controlled by English barons while the centre and the north of the country were dominated by competing Welsh princes. In 1211 John led an army against Llywelyn ap Iorworth, one of the princes who was becoming too powerful, and forced him into submission. However, when it became clear that John planned the complete conquest of Wales, Llywelyn led a national fight back. Many of John's gains were lost while John had to deal with the uprising of the barons in England. However, it is significant that when Henry III came to the throne on John's death Llywelyn did recognise his overlordship.

Supporters of John argue that once the lands in Europe were lost it was right for English kings to start concentrating on Britain. They claim that England could never have held on to the lands in Europe and that the future lay in England establishing its control over the rest of the British Isles. John, they say, was the king who started this policy. You will see that Edward I followed this idea.

When John lost many of his lands in France, including the Channel ports, the need for a proper fleet became crucial for England's defences, especially when the king of France had ideas of invading England.

It is to John's credit that he responded to this need. By 1205 he had a fleet of 46 galleys stationed in 15 different ports from King's Lynn on the east coast, along the south coast, and up the west coast as far as Gloucester. He also had five ships based in Ireland. During the rest of his reign the fleet grew in size (twenty new ships were built between 1209 and 1212). By 1212 the English fleet was in control of the English Channel and was capturing French merchant ships. The importance of John's reforms was clear in 1213 when the French were planning an invasion. The English fleet destroyed the French fleet and the invasion was called off. By the end of John's reign England had emerged as a major naval power – a tradition that was to last for centuries.

Summary task

1   Award John a mark out of 10 for his efforts in each of Scotland, Ireland, Wales and the south coast of England. Briefly explain why you have given him these marks.

2   Overall, how good a king was John?

Here are some good points about him:
- a gifted commander of the army
- provided justice across England
- developed the navy to strengthen England's defences
- extended English control into Ireland, Scotland and Wales
- began building a united Britain

and here are some bad points:
- failed to win loyalty of the barons
- made huge tax demands
- caused a civil war
- lost lands in Europe
- dispute with Pope lost him respect.

Can you think of any more good or bad points? It is up to you to reach your own opinion about him. The ragbag (pages 113–14) might help you.

3a) Construct a timeline for John's reign. Put on it the ten most important events that tell us something about how good a king he was. You will want to think about the following:
- Did he keep the barons happy?
- Did he keep law and order?
- Did he look after the ordinary people?
- Did he defend the country and have military victories?

b)   Then use the timeline to draw a graph to show how well John was doing at different times in his reign. Do this by adding a vertical axis, labelled 1–10, to your timeline and plotting John's 'scores' above each event.

2.2 | *Edward I*

Edward I came to the throne in 1272 already an experienced soldier. He was 30 years old – in his prime. He had huge physical presence. He was impatient, ambitious and could be savage towards his enemies. Once he had made up his mind he was determined to get his own way – he didn't know the meaning of the word 'compromise'.

Discussion point

Would these qualities make Edward a good king?

Some historians claim Edward I had two main aims: to build a great empire by unifying Britain under his authority; and to make the monarchy powerful again after the mistakes of John and Henry III (Edward's father).

Conquering Britain

Edward's reign was dominated by war. He spent much of his reign fighting either in Wales or in Scotland. Because Wales and Scotland were later united with England there is a danger we let this knowledge affect how we view Edward's actions – he can be seen as starting the process of eventual unification and English domination.

Some history books will tell you that Edward invaded Wales and Scotland because of his ambition to control every part of the British Isles. They argue that once King John had lost many of the English monarchy's lands on the continent, the focus was bound to change to the creation of a united British kingdom under English rule. They also claim that Edward realised the way to keep the loyalty of the barons was to keep them involved in building a great empire. Edward's empire was to be Britain. Did Edward start out with such a master plan or did he simply react to situations and problems as they arose? Had he lost all interest in the English lands on the continent? You will also see that Edward's actions in Wales and Scotland had very different results. Why was Edward more successful in Wales than in Scotland?

Success in Wales

The background

Wales had been divided into several kingdoms but in 1267 Llywelyn ap Gruffydd was recognised as 'Prince of Wales' by Henry III. As part of the agreement Llywelyn had to do homage to Henry as his overlord and pay him £16,600 in ten instalments. But for all practical purposes Llywelyn was an independent ruler. However, Llywelyn did not control all of Wales. William the Conqueror had many years before given the borderlands (called the Marches) between England and Wales to some of his barons. Over the next 200 years these barons and their families had conquered parts of Wales for themselves. As you can see from Source 1, by the time Edward I became king, Llywelyn's stronghold was in the north-west of Wales but he also controlled much of the west. English barons controlled most of the rest of Wales.

● **SOURCE 1**

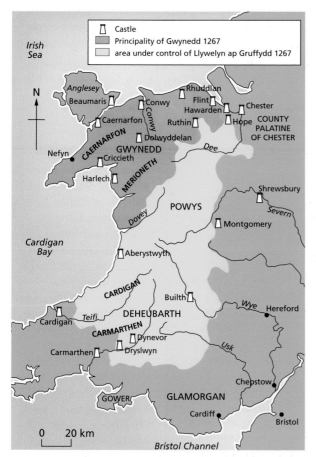

Wales at the time of Edward's conquests.

Tension between Edward and Llywelyn

For the first eight years of his reign much of Edward's attention was turned towards Wales.

When Edward became king Llywelyn refused to do homage and recognise Edward as his overlord. He also stopped paying the annual instalments. This was bound to annoy Edward who was determined to teach him a lesson. He also remembered the civil war of his father's reign and knew that he had to assert his authority. Critics of Llywelyn say he was getting too big for his boots and was over-confident.

However, Llywelyn was also angry with Edward because Edward was protecting Llywelyn's brother Dafydd. Dafydd had tried to assassinate him and had fled to Edward when the attempt failed. If Llywelyn let his brother get away with the assassination attempt he would lose all credibility.

Llywelyn was in a weak position. His position as the Prince of Wales had only recently been created and he was not part of the European royal network (the Scottish kings were), and he was trying to create a unified Wales that had never before existed. To do this he needed to impose himself and to collect money, and this often alienated many of the Welsh. (In fact some of the Welsh lords and 9000 of their followers fought on Edward's side.) On top of this, Llywelyn had the English lords to deal with, who were gradually taking more and more Welsh land.

The First War of 1277

In 1277 Edward lost his patience and launched a well-planned campaign. Three enormous armies moved into Wales. They headed for Gwynedd in the north-west which was Llywelyn's power base. At the same time Edward's fleet took Anglesey. Llywelyn was trapped in Snowdonia and had no choice but to agree to peace terms that reduced his power. Edward consolidated his control of north and west Wales by building castles at Flint, Rhuddlan, Ruthin, Builth and Aberystwyth.

The Second War of 1282–83

Relations between Llywelyn and Edward were good for a while. However, unrest was growing. Edward's officials were upsetting the Welsh people by ignoring Welsh laws and customs. As Edward's castles were gradually being completed it looked as if Edward's grip over Wales was getting firmer and Llywelyn's power was fading. Dafydd reacted first. Soon Edward had a full-scale rebellion on his hands and Llywelyn had no choice but to join in. Edward threw everything he had at the Welsh who had little chance against his enormous army. The rebellion faltered when Llywelyn was killed at the end of 1282. His head was displayed on the Tower of London.

Edward took his revenge by burning Welsh villages and taking the men as hostages. When Dafydd was captured in the following year he was made an example of: he was dragged by horses to the scaffold, hanged alive, his bowels were burned out and then his body was quartered. His head joined his brother's on the Tower of London.

Edward triumphant

Just fifteen years after the English had recognised Llywelyn as Prince of Wales, Edward had ended Welsh independence and had control of Wales.

Keeping control

To make sure he kept control of Wales, Edward built more castles – Caernarfon, Conwy, Harlech and Beaumaris – as well as strengthening existing ones. Edward's castles were major achievements. They were built to fit perfectly the geographical features of their sites and many could be relieved from the sea in case there was a siege. They symbolised English rule and were effective as a deterrent – none of them fell until Owain Glyndwr's rebellion over a hundred years later.

● **SOURCE 2**

An engraving of Conwy Castle from 1825.

Edward also ensured control by making sure that Wales was governed properly. New Welsh counties were created and every one was put under the control of a sheriff. A new system of courts was set up and English law was introduced. However, Edward was sensible enough to realise that the Welsh were best governed by the Welsh and many of the officials appointed were locals.

How did Edward's castles work?

Remember the purpose of the castles was to keep Wales under control. So how did they do this?

One of Edward's most impressive castles is Harlech. It took seven and a half years to build and cost £9,500 – an enormous sum in those days. You can see from Source 3 how the builders have exploited the site's natural advantages. The castle is built on a high promontory with views as far as Snowdonia in the distance. From its high position it could see, and control, the main supply routes. This made it possible to see approaching attackers long before they arrived at the castle. Its high position also made it more difficult to attack and easier to defend.

● **SOURCE 3**

Enormous round towers – round towers are much stronger than square ones. The castle was built from the same rock on which it stands. The towers project from the wall allowing defenders to cover the walls. The defences were very flexible. Towers could be manned or abandoned, connected or isolated as circumstance required.

Because three sides of the castle are protected by the sea, the only way to attack it was from the east. Attackers from land would first see the massive gatehouse protecting this side of the castle. The gatehouse has three portcullises and is the main defensive feature – almost impossible to attack successfully.

Arrow slits allowed archers to fire at attackers while they themselves remained protected.

Harlech is a concentric castle. It has two rows of walls, one inside the other. If attackers broke through the outer wall, they still faced the inner wall. The inner wall is massive and much higher than the outer so the archers could fire their arrows from both walls. The ground in-between the walls was called 'the killing ground' because if attackers were trapped here they could be killed easily.

Harlech even had an extra wall at the bottom of the cliff.

Harlech Castle.

If you visit the castle today you will find that the sea has receded but in Edward's time the waves lapped the cliffs beneath the castle. If the castle was under siege it could be supported by soldiers and supplies from the sea, or if the siege got too bad the sea provided an escape route for the inhabitants.

Harlech Castle worked in other ways as well. Firstly, it was one of a chain of castles that ringed the north-west of Wales. These castles were designed to keep Llywelyn and his army in the mountains and to ensure that the rebellion could never spread to the rest of Wales.

Castles were not meant just to be difficult to attack, they were also designed to control the local people and the local area. Remember, Edward wanted to keep Wales and the Welsh under control. The heavily armed soldiers in the castle could ride ten miles there and ten miles back in a day. This put a large area directly under the control of the castle. If an enemy wanted to control the local area they would have to take the castle first.

Edward built towns and villages near to his castles. Here the local population lived under the powerful gaze of the castle. After Edward's victory the Welsh were treated as second class citizens. For example, they were not allowed to carry arms or have strangers stay overnight. The castle was also a centre of government. The king's judges, tax collectors and civil servants would all be based in the castle, allowing Edward's control to spread out across the Welsh countryside.

Failure in Scotland

Edward: overlord of Scotland?

The thirteenth century had been a period of peace between England and Scotland and there was much intermarriage between the two royal families. When he became king, Edward had no plans to conquer Scotland. However, like other English kings, he had no doubt that he had overlordship of Scotland and that the Scottish lords owed him allegiance. English kings also needed to keep an eye on Scotland in case it allied with England's enemy France.

The situation changed in 1286 when the Scottish king Alexander was killed when he fell from his horse, tumbled down a cliff and broke his neck. His heir was his six-year-old granddaughter Margaret, 'Maid of Norway'. A marriage was arranged between her and Edward's son. Edward hoped this would help him have influence over Scotland. However, Margaret died before the marriage could take place. Several people claimed the right to be the next king and the Scots asked Edward's help in choosing who it should be. John Balliol was chosen but was soon in dispute with Edward over how far Scotland was independent from England. John gave in when Edward, in one of his blood-curdling tirades, threatened to confiscate John's castles and imprison him. The Scots were so angry at this that they got rid of John as king and made a treaty with Edward's enemy Philip IV of France.

A quick conquest!

By 1296 war was inevitable. Edward used the same tactics as in Wales. He took a huge army (some 26,000 men) and simply planned to smash the Scots. An idea of his tactics can be got from what he did to Berwick where he had 11,000 people slaughtered including many women and children. This was a warning to the rest of Scotland and a few weeks later Edward's army had completely trampled over the Scots. Edward got what he wanted – the Scots recognised him as their overlord (it seems he had no interest in ruling Scotland directly as king).

● **SOURCE 4**

A photograph of the William Wallace monument in Dryburgh.

William Wallace to the rescue

However, some Scots were not going to be defeated so easily. They wanted an independent Scotland. When William Wallace led a rising against English rule the whole of Scotland seemed to rise up to support him. At first Edward, busy fighting the French, took little notice of the problems in Scotland, until the Scots defeated the English army at Stirling Bridge in 1297. Over the next seven years Edward poured enormous resources into Scotland and although he had some small wins he never managed an outright victory.

The Scots cleverly avoided big battles and used guerrilla hit-and-run tactics. In this they were helped by the mountains of the Highland region. Edward thought he could win simply by the use of brute force – he showed little tactical or strategic skill. He also failed to win over enough Scots to his side. This was partly because many of them were determined never to be ruled by the English, but also because Edward failed to give them enough land to persuade them.

In 1305 William Wallace was captured. A show trial found him guilty of not obeying Edward as his overlord. Edward had him dragged through the streets of London and then hanged, disembowelled while still alive and executed. His innards were then burned. His head was stuck on a pike on London Bridge, and his arms and legs were sent to Newcastle, Berwick, Perth and Aberdeen for all to see.

Robert Bruce takes over

By 1305 an uneasy truce had developed. Just as things were quietening down Edward made it clear that as far as he was concerned the Scottish monarchy had been abolished and that Scotland was now merely one of his 'lands'. Robert Bruce immediately rebelled. Bruce had earlier come over to Edward's side and could have probably been won over with the offer of lands or the Scottish throne. However, Edward made an enemy of him by offering him nothing and in 1306 he was crowned as king of Scotland by his supporters.

As the war dragged on Edward reacted with more cruelty, hanging, drawing and quartering all prisoners. But this simply increased Scottish support for Bruce and when Edward died in 1307 he left his son Edward II a difficult problem in Scotland. This was to lead to a famous Scottish victory at the Battle of Bannockburn and eventually Robert Bruce being recognised by England as the rightful king of Scotland.

Discussion point

How well did Edward I deal with Scotland? Did he have bad luck or make bad mistakes?

Edward I and the development of Parliament

The normal pattern across the Middle Ages was cooperation between king and barons. This suited everybody much better than conflict. However, each side kept a wary eye on the other. For most of his reign Edward was in charge. He was firm and ungenerous towards the nobles but rarely did anything unfair or stupid enough to annoy them as a group. He kept them in their place and made sure their powers did not grow; he was determined he would not have a repeat of his father's reign. However, he did include bishops, judges and barons in his council as earlier kings had done. He never repeated his father's mistake of pushing the barons out and replacing them with his favourites. As a result Edward never lost the respect of the barons.

First ideas of a Parliament

Edward's father Henry III ran into trouble with the barons when he started to give land, castles and jobs to his foreign favourites. They were especially annoyed when he did not use them as his main advisers. A civil war followed with the barons being led by Simon de Montfort. The barons forced Henry to sack his favourites, and set up a council of 15 barons who would have the final say over the choice of the king's ministers and the spending of money. Another civil war followed and in 1265 Simon de Montfort called a Parliament that included not just the barons but elected knights from the shires and burgesses from some towns. Simon eventually lost the war. But the idea of having elected commoners in Parliament would return.

Money needed for wars

Medieval kings had to pay for very expensive wars. At first they paid for them by the money they made from their own lands. But Edward, who was fighting a war in nearly every year of his reign, needed much more money. At first he got groups like merchants to agree to pay a tax, but he then realised it would be better to gather representatives of everyone together. They could then agree to pay a tax on behalf of everyone in the country. This meant Edward could tax everyone. Edward only called a Parliament when he wanted money and as you will see Parliament did not always agree to a tax. A further development was made in 1297 when Edward was forced to agree that he could only levy a tax if Parliament agreed to it.

● **SOURCE 5**

The Lords: about 100 landowners and bishops

The Commons: 230 (2 elected from each county and 2 elected from each larger town).

We are much more important than the common people. The king only calls them because he wants money from them.

If you want any money from us, we want our grievances dealt with first.

Edward's first Parliament.

The development of Parliament can be seen as a weakening of the monarchy and the beginnings of democracy. This is not what was happening. Parliament actually opened up a new source of money for the king. He could now tax the population as a whole because their representatives agreed to it. In return he would listen to their complaints and sometimes do something about them. Parliament did develop further powers in his son's reign but this was because Edward II was such a weak king. If there had been another powerful king like Edward I it might not have developed in the same way.

Reasons why Parliament did not bring democracy:

- It remained under the king's control – he called it when he wanted some money.
- The idea for any laws it passed came from him.
- The Lords was much more important than the Commons.
- The King's Council still met and this is where important decisions were made.

Discussion point

Do you think the development of Parliament had weakened the monarchy or made it stronger?

Edward's impact on everyday lives

One way in which a medieval king affected the lives of ordinary people was how well he provided peace and law and order. Edward was determined to be a strong king and ensure that the civil wars that plagued his father's reign were not repeated. In this he was successful and the disorder, violence and plunder of a civil war were avoided. For this everyone would have been grateful.

Edward also hated corruption and injustice, especially when carried out by his own officials. In 1274 he ordered a massive investigation to find out if there was good government in all parts of the country. He knew that crime had grown in the chaos of his father's reign. All over the country, juries were questioned about this. The findings were worrying – Henry's officials were guilty of corruption and misgovernment and the system of law and order was not working well.

Edward made efforts to put this right by the Statute of Westminster (1275) and other laws passed over the next fifteen years. Attempts were made to deal with officials who were filling their own pockets and extorting money from people. (For example, when they seized food for Edward's army or collected taxes, they took more than they should and kept the extra for themselves.) Existing laws were enforced to try and make sure that the systems of watch and hue and cry were working properly. All areas, known as hundreds, were reminded of their responsibilities to detect and stop crime. Although not perfect, these measures probably made the everyday lives of most people a little easier and more secure.

We know that Edward did not solve all these problems because later in his reign there were more complaints about royal officials and in 1298 another inquiry was set up.

Edward and the Jews

One group of people who definitely did not benefit from Edward's rule were England's Jews. It is easy today to condemn out of hand the way Edward treated the Jews, but we have to remember that Edward was a man of his time. He had the same attitudes, prejudices and values of people then and we cannot expect him to act like someone from the 21st century. This does not mean that what he did was right; it means we have to view him in context.

Jews settled in England soon after the Norman Conquest in 1066, many of them fleeing from persecution in Europe. They were obviously different from everybody else. They spoke a different language, and they were not Christians – they did not believe that Jesus Christ was the son of God.

Laws in England made them even more different. They were not allowed to own land or enter a trade, but they were allowed to lend money at interest. Christians were not allowed to do this. Many Jews became successful money lenders and the money they lent kings contributed to building great cathedrals and fighting wars. Unfortunately it also led to a lot of people owing the Jews money and resenting the fact. English kings also made money by taxing Jews heavily.

Gradually the treatment of the Jews got worse. In 1190 there was a bloody massacre of Jewish men, women and children in York.

Edward's persecution of Jews was a consistent policy that developed through his reign. In 1275 he banned the lending of money at interest (the only way of making a living open to Jews). He also ordered that all Jews should wear yellow badges so they could be identified. He then blamed Jews for the illegal clipping of coins (shaving off a small portion of coins to melt down and reuse for profit). He had 290 Jews executed, and fined many more. In 1290 he went one step further and ordered that all Jews leave the country. They were given three months to go and any that had not left by then would be put to death.

Why did Edward do this? Was it his religious beliefs or more selfish motives that drove him?

> Edward shared the views of his time. He also was a pious Christian and no doubt thought he was doing the right thing.

> The Church had been putting pressure on Edward to act against the Jews and he certainly wanted to keep the Church on his side.

> He also wanted money for his wars and it was no coincidence that in the same year as he expelled the Jews, the Church and Parliament had agreed to pay him enormous amounts in taxes. Edward also owed Jews a lot of money – now he had expelled them, he would not have to pay it back.

> Edward knew that acting against the Jews would be very popular. In fact historians have argued that the expulsion of the Jews was the most popular thing Edward ever did. Edward was always on the look out to raise money, and if he could win popularity as well, why not?

Edward's last years: a sour ending?

The year 1290 seems to have been a turning point in Edward's reign. It was then that his wife Eleanor died, and Edward was never the same again. In fact there is a sense that his whole reign was never the same again. All his major successes were behind him and he seemed to pay less attention to running the country.

His victories over the Welsh were in the past and his troubles with Scotland were just beginning. In 1294 war with France started, a war that was to last until 1298. In these years Edward was constantly torn between problems in Scotland and problems in France. There was to be no great victory in France and eventually the war fizzled out as Edward ran out of money.

It was also at this time that there was a series of bad harvests, which put food prices up and caused great hardship. This was made worse by Edward's officials seizing food and collecting taxes for his wars. This went on year after year and led to much complaining and grumbling. Edward was becoming less popular.

His wars were doing the damage. It was because of war that he began to neglect justice and good government. It was because of the wars that in 1297 his officials seized all the money people had deposited in churches for safe-keeping. It was because he needed men for his armies that he gave criminals pardons if they signed up. Edward's wars were putting an enormous strain on the country and were causing great hardship.

In 1297 these problems boiled over. Taxes had become so heavy that Parliament refused to agree to any more. In reply, Edward started to levy taxes without getting agreement for them. This caused a lot of unrest and people started to refuse to pay the taxes. When Edward called for the barons to support him in his war in France, not one went with him! When he sailed for France in 1297 the country appeared to be on the verge of civil war.

Edward was saved by the Scots. Their victory at Stirling Bridge over Edward's army created a sense of national unity in England and the barons rallied round to help the king defeat the Scots. The crisis was over but at a price. Edward had to agree to confirm the clauses of Magna Carta, and to agree that all future taxes would require the agreement of Parliament. To avoid further trouble over taxes in the last years of his reign, Edward borrowed large amounts of money, leaving his son huge debts.

Edward's legacy

Edward was a strong king who was feared and respected but not loved. His son's reign was a disaster – how far was Edward to blame for this? What kind of legacy did he leave his son?

Discussion point

As he was dying Edward asked that his body should be boiled until the bones were clean of flesh, and that his skeleton should be carried north on every expedition against the Scots. What does this tell us about Edward?

Summary task

1   Overall, how good a king was Edward I?

Good points

- He restored the prestige of the monarchy after his father's reign.
- He conquered Wales.
- There was no civil war.
- He found a new source of money – general taxation.
- His son's succession was peaceful.

Bad points

- He fought very expensive wars and left his son huge debts.
- He was not successful in France or Scotland and the war with Scotland was still going on when he died.
- Lawlessness was increasing; he started another major campaign against it in 1305 because it was so bad.
- He had lost some of his power to Parliament.

2   Can you think of any more good or bad points?

3a)   Construct a timeline for Edward's reign. Put on it the ten most important events that tell us something about how good a king he was. You will want to think about the following:

- Did he keep the barons happy?
- Did he keep law and order?
- Did he look after the ordinary people?
- Did he defend the country and have military victories?

b)   Then use the timeline to draw a graph to show how well Edward was doing at different times in his reign. Do this by adding a vertical axis, labelled 1–10, to your timeline and plotting Edward's 'scores' above each event.

Henry V

Read this recent judgement from a historian.

● **SOURCE 1**

Henry V is often regarded as one of England's finest kings. In English myth he is the ideal Englishman: plucky and persevering, austere and audacious, cool-headed, stiff-lipped and effortlessly superior. A saintly king, a true king, crowned by God. A warrior-king, helmed and mounted. Yet Henry's kingship was tainted. His dynasty had no right to the crown. His victories were triumphs of hype, stained by blood of war crimes. His holiness was remarkable, especially in his zeal for burning heretics, but a saint he ain't.

Adapted from 'The Myth of Henry V' on www.bbc.co.uk/history.

This suggests that Henry V might not be the great king he is often depicted as. His victories in France are famous and writers in Henry's own time wrote about nothing else. Therefore it might be a good idea to examine first Henry's record back in England. Did he govern the country well, or did he, as some historians claim, neglect it for the more exciting pastime of fighting in France?

Did Henry neglect England?

Henry V spent less than half of his reign in England, and much of that time was spent in preparing for war in France. It could be dangerous for a king to leave his country and go abroad. There was always the possibility of a rebellion with a disgruntled nobleman trying to take the throne. To this we have to add the fact that Henry IV's reign had been very unstable. He had faced a series of revolts by nobles, a rebellion in Wales and war with Scotland. All this seems to suggest that Henry V would be very unwise to leave England for long.

When Henry came to the throne the country was plagued with lawlessness. There were many complaints about robbers and thieves, and riots and disorders. In Henry's first Parliament in 1413 the Commons petitioned the new king to suppress lawlessness throughout his lands. Although Henry's main aim was to win back lands in France, he clearly decided that he could not leave England without dealing with the law and order problem first.

This was not going to be an easy job. Henry had no police force and no permanent army. To do what the Commons wanted he would have to rely on local communities – mainly the nobles and gentry, but also the peasants who served on juries. However, these local communities could be very suspicious of what they regarded as interference from outside. If they closed ranks and refused to cooperate there was little a king could do.

As soon as he became king, Henry started a strong campaign of law enforcement. Special commissions of inquiry were sent out to many parts of the country to deal with crimes and disturbances.

In **Shropshire** and **Staffordshire** the Earl of Arundel and the local gentry were a law unto themselves. Supported by armed bands they extorted money and property, and fought each other. They were difficult to deal with because they were the very people that Henry depended on to run the localities. He used a mixture of firmness and generosity. Many had to hand over huge sums of money as a guarantee of their future good behaviour while others had to win their way back into royal favour by fighting for the king in France.

In the summer of 1414 there were many complaints of disorder in the **Midlands**. Henry made a real effort to deal with this but there were soon thousands of cases waiting to go to court. Henry gave up and issued a general pardon in return for a tax. Those pardoned (about 5000 in the next three years) included murderers and rapists.

Public order had never been properly restored in the **Welsh Marches** (the borderlands between England and Wales) after Owain Glyndwr's rebellion in Henry's father's reign. In 1413 Henry sent the Earl of Arundel to hear former rebels ask for pardons and swear their loyalty to the king – over 600 did so and there was no more trouble. Henry also wanted to bring justice to the people of Wales so he sent judges there to deal with disorder and corrupt officials. Officials guilty of extortion (forcing people to give money) and embezzlement (using public money for themselves) were sacked. Henry's policy in Wales worked: huge numbers of Welshmen signed up for Henry's armies.

ENGLAND

WALES

N

0   200 km

When the King's judges went down to **Devon** in January 1414 to deal with piracy they were obstructed by the local community and achieved nothing.

In 1415, a plan to rebel in the North and assassinate Henry as he left for France from **Southampton** failed. The ringleaders were swiftly executed.

In April 1414 efforts to stop the activities of pirates in the **English Channel** failed.

Discussion point

Using the information around this map, discuss how successful Henry was in dealing with problems of disorder.

Law and order was not perfect for the rest of the reign but Henry's policies seem to have worked because there was little serious trouble in England during his long absences in France. You have probably noticed that all of these problems that Henry was trying to deal with were at the beginning of the reign. This tells us that these were problems left over from his father's reign and that Henry acted to deal with them very quickly. He was trying to ensure the country was stable, so that he could embark on his great adventure in France.

Henry and the nobles

A much greater danger to Henry than minor disturbances around the country were the great nobles of the realm. If they wanted to, they could unseat a king. This is what had happened to Edward II and Richard II. Henry's father Henry IV had led a revolt of noblemen to topple Richard II and take the throne. Once he was king he had had to defeat several rebellions. Two of these, by the Welsh and by the powerful Percy family, took place towards the end of Henry IV's reign, showing that this threat remained.

These troubles had meant that some nobles ended up on the losing side and had lost their titles and estates. In Henry V's reign, they were keen to regain what they had lost and if he did not deal with them they might rebel.

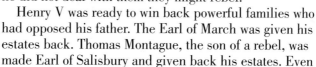

> How do I deal with powerful nobles?

Henry V was ready to win back powerful families who had opposed his father. The Earl of March was given his estates back. Thomas Montague, the son of a rebel, was made Earl of Salisbury and given back his estates. Even the powerful Percy family were brought back in from the cold. Henry Percy, whose father had fought against Henry in the Battle of Shrewsbury in 1403, was married to link him to Henry's family, and later made Earl of Northumberland. Henry obviously believed that it was better to have powerful families such as these on his side. The policy worked as they became his close supporters.

Henry also created strong personal ties with many of the leading nobles. This was helped by the fact that most of them were in their twenties when Henry himself was 26 years old. They fought together so often in France that a sense of brotherhood was created between them. It is significant that most of the leading nobles went with Henry on his expeditions to France. Henry had charisma, was a gifted military commander, and won the nobles' respect and devotion. They were proud to be contributing to England's achievements; of course, the fact that Henry was successful in his battles helped a lot.

The wars in France created plenty of opportunities for the nobles to make a lot of money through booty and ransoms. Henry also rewarded them with estates in France.

Despite creating close ties with many of the nobles Henry always emphasised his own royal dignity and expected his position to be respected. He was never 'one of the lads'. He was a firm disciplinarian and dealt harshly with anyone who let him down. He had no favourites. He dealt with the nobles evenly and fairly and gave no one reason to be jealous. He did not try to threaten or exploit them. He trusted them and they trusted him.

Discussion point

Name three things Henry did to improve relations with the nobles.

One group Henry had to deal with almost immediately were the Lollards. They were a religious group who rejected some of the beliefs of the Christian Church. They also believed that ordinary people should be able to read the Bible for themselves. They translated the Bible into English and printed and distributed it. This worried the government because the Bible contained ideas that could make people question the nature of society and authority at the time. Henry had very strong but totally traditional religious beliefs, and so he was determined to see the Lollards dealt with.

In 1414 Sir John Oldcastle organised a Lollard rebellion. His followers were to meet outside **London**, and then capture the king. The rebellion was a miserable failure and Henry had the ringleaders swiftly executed. The activities of the Lollards were investigated up and down the country but Henry later issued a general pardon to avoid provoking any more trouble. He had taken quick and decisive action, which reassured everyone.

Case study: The Battle of Agincourt

Henry's struggle for the French throne was the single most important aspect of his reign. Medieval kings were expected to be soldiers. A king who was successful in battle (especially against the old enemy of France) was likely to be seen as a great king. Henry led armies to France on three occasions, in 1415, 1417 and 1421. His most famous victory was at the Battle of Agincourt in 1415.

The background

You will remember that in 1204 King John had lost most of the lands that the English monarchy held in France. In 1328 when Charles IV of France died, Edward III claimed the French throne because his mother was Charles' sister.

In 1337 the Hundred Years War between England and France began. Edward III had spectacular victories at the battles of Crécy and Poitiers. However, after he died in 1377, the French won back some territory. During the troubled years of Richard II and Henry IV, England could not afford to be active in France. However, Henry V was determined to win back the French throne and the lands in France he thought were rightfully his.

Negotiations

Henry negotiated with France and prepared for war at the same time. Some historians have said this is an example of his dishonesty while others have said it was simply common sense.

In the negotiations, Henry demanded the throne of France, but said he would accept instead Normandy, Touraine, Anjou, Maine, Brittany and Flanders! He also wanted one million six hundred crowns and marriage with Catherine, the French king's daughter. This marriage was important to him because it would give his heirs a proper claim to French lands he conquered. The French were convinced that Henry was not serious in these demands and was simply posturing. Henry brought the negotiations to an end and continued to prepare for war.

Why did Henry win the Battle of Agincourt?

Preparing for war

Wars are not just won on the battlefield. The preparations beforehand are just as important. Henry understood this. He had started by sorting out law and order in England. He now had to make more direct preparations for war. You can see from these preparations the enormous care that was taken. The smallest detail was looked after.

- Between 1414 and 1420 eight different taxes were granted by Parliament with scarcely a murmur of protest. Henry got more money with less trouble than any other English king.

- Castles on England's northern border were repaired and strengthened.

- The coastal defences of towns like Portsmouth and Southampton were strengthened.

- The selling of bows, arrows and artillery to the Scots and other foreign countries was banned.

- In 1413, 12,000 arrows were ordered (archers fired about 15 arrows a minute; this was only the first of many such orders).

- Sheriffs were ordered to find 1,190,000 goose feathers. (What do you think these were for?)

- All able-bodied men between the ages of 16 and 60 had to practise archery every Sunday.

- Orders for cannon went out – these were made all round the country and had to be hauled overland to London (they could be moved about 7 miles a day). The amount of work involved in providing the cannon can be seen if you remember that 248 cannon were needed for one siege, as well as the cannonballs weighing 150 pounds each, 30,000 pounds of gunpowder, 5,000 sacks of charcoal, plus bellows, carts and horses.

- The export of gunpowder was banned.

- Hundreds of blacksmiths, stonemasons, carpenters, sawyers and joiners were recruited to go on the expedition.

- Orders to collect as much copper, brass, bronze and iron as possible were issued.

- Furnaces all over London were used to make armour, weapons, nails, horseshoes and tools.

- Hundreds of oxen, bullocks and cows were bought.

- Henry inherited a fleet of six ships. He increased this to twelve by 1415 and also hired 630 ships from Holland. All large ships between the River Thames and Newcastle-upon-Tyne were also seized by the king's men.

- Bow-makers were hired and thousands of bow-staves purchased.

- The defences of Calais (which still belonged to England) were strengthened. Orders were issued that all houses had to be roofed with slate or tiles and not thatch.

- Enormous numbers of arms and supplies including huge amounts of salted beef, pork and wine were stored in Calais.

Henry sets sail

The army of 12,000 men gathered at Southampton. On 11 August 1415 Henry's fleet set sail for France. About 700 ships carried the soldiers; workmen with their tools and equipment; cattle; and enormous amounts of food, horses, cannon, armour, weapons, carts and siege engines. The fleet dropped anchor off the Normandy coast and by 17 August the entire army had landed. The first objective was to lay siege to the town of Harfleur.

Dysentery strikes

The siege took eighteen days, rather longer than Henry had been expecting. Then dysentery struck. This was caused by food or water being infected by human faeces. It caused bloody diarrhoea and was a killer. Given the number of men and horses, and the poor sanitary arrangements, it is not surprising this happened. By the time the siege was over, Henry had lost over 25 per cent of his army to the disease.

● **SOURCE 2**

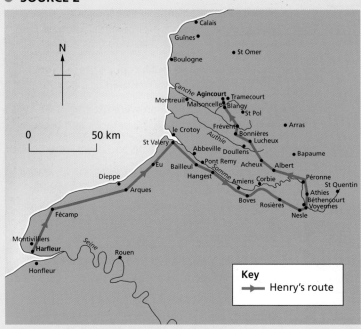

A map of northern France showing Henry's route from Harfleur to Agincourt.

The march to Calais

Henry had a decision to make. His army was a shadow of what it had been – there were 900 men-at-arms and 5000 archers left. He could go home, having established a bridgehead for a future invasion, or he could raid and plunder his way south-west down to Aquitaine. However, neither of these options would do much to help him win the throne of France.

So instead, against the views of his noblemen, Henry decided to march to Calais. This meant marching through Normandy which he claimed belonged to him and he would not be far from the French army at Rouen. Historians have tried to work out why he did this. Was he trying to draw the French into a decisive battle? Was he confident that a small well-trained army like his could defeat a much larger one?

Henry ensured that his small army stayed together, that no one strayed off for a bit of plunder. Discipline was all important. They had problems crossing the River Somme as the obvious crossing places were well defended. As they moved deeper into the heart of France they were getting no closer to Calais. Henry's soldiers were growing weary, and rations were so low that they had to eat hazelnuts from the hedgerows. Eventually they managed to cross the Somme and they plodded on in rain and cold winds. They then came across the French army barring their way at Agincourt.

Ready for action

The two armies drew up opposite each other and waited. As darkness fell they were so close that the English soldiers could hear the voices of the French. Henry ordered complete silence so the French did not know their exact positions. This would prevent a surprise attack in the night. It was so quiet that the French thought the English had slipped away. That night it rained in torrents, the men were soaked and their armour was in danger from rust. Henry sent out a group of knights to scout the battlefield so that he could make his final plans. They told him that the rain had turned the battlefield into a mudbath. Henry realised this would slow the French infantry and cavalry down and make them easy targets for his archers. Although Henry was making good use of the night before the battle, the one thing he did not do was the one thing he is famous for! He did not make the famous speech that you read on page 71.

● **SOURCE 3**

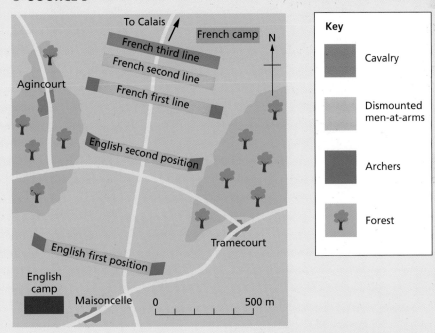

A plan of the armies before the battle.

The two sides were about 800 metres apart, separated by a gently rolling recently ploughed field that had turned into a mudbath. A slight dip in the field meant that the two sides could clearly see each other. On either side of the field was a forest. The field narrowed to only 800 metres where the armies would meet. The French army was about 36,000 (4000 of them archers) strong while the English army had almost 6,000 men (5000 of them archers).

Henry put all his soldiers into a single line. There were no reserves. This was very unusual and a big risk but Henry clearly decided he did not have enough men to keep some back. The line was divided into three groups of soldiers. Each of these groups was made up of the advance, the main body and the rearguard, each about four deep. The archers were on each flank of the army protected by large stakes. Some historians also think that there were archers in between the groups of soldiers.

The French formed three lines. The front two were made up of dismounted soldiers. In the third line the men were on horseback. The cavalry was placed on each flank. Between the first and second lines were archers and crossbowmen.

What happened in the battle?

● SOURCE 4

A nineteenth-century copy of a medieval illustration of the Battle of Agincourt. Henry is shown, on horseback, leading the English army.

The English advance

For four hours the two armies stared at each other. The inferior numbers of the English would put them at a great disadvantage if they attacked. While the French did not fancy wading through the mud! Or perhaps the French were waiting for the English to run out of food and they would win without having to fight. Henry rode up and down his lines encouraging his men to do their best. He also told them a lie – that the French had boasted they would cut off two fingers from the right hand of every English archer. When the battle started Henry fought in the centre of the battle to inspire his men.

Henry knew that without food his troops would get weaker and so at about 11 a.m. he ordered his men to advance. They moved forward steadily until the French were just within the range of their longbows. If the French had attacked while the English were advancing, and before they had reset their positions, the English would have been in trouble. Henry then ordered the archers to drive their stakes into the ground at an angle that would ensure the French horses were impaled on them. Henry planned to provoke the French into attacking. He ordered the archers to fire. They could fire ten flights a minute and the air was soon thick with arrows pouring down on the French cavalry.

The French attack

Henry's plan worked. The French cavalry on the flanks attacked the English archers on the flanks. It was a disaster for the French. Their cavalry charged at about 12 miles an hour while flight after flight of arrows hit them. The arrows were not strong enough to penetrate the knight's armour but the horses were not so well protected. Wounded horses threw their riders into the mud. Others crashed into the English stakes. As the survivors retreated they crashed into their own soldiers who were advancing.

Everything was going wrong for the French. Their horses had churned up the mud making it harder for later attacks. The forest narrowed the field, squeezing the French against each other and preventing them from outflanking the English. The French attack was chaotic. The French noblemen rushed like an undisciplined mob to be in the front line. They were jostling each other and they had no room to lift their weapons. All this time the English archers were firing at them. The French had so little room that they could not fire their artillery – because of the chaos, they were just as likely to kill each other as they were the English.

By the time the French reached the English lines they were exhausted by the mud, the over-crowding and the arrows. The English lines were soon protected by a solid wall of French bodies! The French soldiers were pushed out towards the English archers who finished them off. Two of them would attack a French knight from the front while a third archer slashed at the unprotected parts behind the knee. They finished him off by thrusting their sword through the grille of his faceplate. Many of the French knights were simply stuck in the mud and were trampled on.

The end

After just half an hour the first two French lines had been destroyed. The English soldiers started to take prisoners for ransom and strip valuables from the dead. Henry, however, wanted all his men ready for a French counter-attack. He knew that there were more French soldiers in their third line than there were in the whole English army. So he ordered all the prisoners to be killed. The French counter-attack failed and the Battle of Agincourt was over. Six thousand French soldiers had been killed and many more taken prisoner.

Task

How far was the victory due to Henry? You can probably find examples of where Henry contributed to the victory. Here are some other reasons for the victory:

- mistakes by the French
- bad luck
- the skill and professionalism of the English soldiers (especially the archers).

Can you find examples of these factors?

Assessing Henry

The death of Henry

When Henry arrived back in London a month later there were huge celebrations to welcome him. At that moment he must have been more popular than an English king has ever been. A mood of euphoria seems to have swept the country.

Henry completed the conquest of Normandy in another expedition in 1417–19. In 1420 in the Treaty of Troyes the French king recognised Henry as his heir as King of France. He also married his daughter to Henry. Henry had achieved one other thing. He came to the throne with many people not convinced he was the rightful king. His victories showed that God was on his side and people recognised him as the rightful king.

Henry returned to France in 1421 to reassert his authority but died the following year from dysentery. The French king, Charles VI, died seven weeks later. If Henry had lived for that long he would have achieved his greatest ambition and become King of France.

Arguments against Henry

Some historians argue that Henry was a lucky king, and that he left a bitter legacy. See if you agree with the points they make.

1 Things were going sour even before Henry died

By the 1420s the country was getting tired of war, and in particular having to pay for it. When Henry asked Parliament for more money there was some opposition and a lot of grumbling. Henry was already heavily in debt and this got worse when he resorted to loans. There was a feeling in Parliament that as Henry's claim to the French throne had been recognised there was no longer the need for war. Many also felt no longer under an obligation to pay taxes for more war. When Henry died the country had enormous debts.

2 Henry was very lucky

During his reign France was divided into warring factions. The king, Charles VI, had periodic bouts of insanity when he was incapable of governing the country. There were power struggles between him, the Dukes of Burgundy and later the Dauphin (the king's eldest son). The decision of the Duke of Burgundy not to support Charles VI was crucial to Henry's success.

3 Henry left the country stuck with an expensive war

When Henry V died he left England with an expensive war it could never win and which it could not afford. While Henry VI was a child the Duke of Bedford felt duty bound to fight for the young king's inheritance in France. But it ended in disaster – by 1450 all that England had left in France was the port of Calais!

4 Did the Treaty of Troyes really mean much?

This treaty was only an agreement with one of the factions in France. It was rejected by the Dauphin and by many regions of France. How were English kings going to make their right to be kings of France a reality? This could only be done by complete conquest of France and that was never possible.

5 Henry made the Wars of the Roses possible

Henry left as his heir a young baby. With no grown-up heir he should have been more careful with his own life. While Henry VI was a child the English nobles began to squabble over who should have power. By the 1450s England was plunged into civil war. In 1461 Henry VI was deposed and Edward, Duke of York became King Edward IV. The Wars of the Roses were underway.

Arguments in his favour

Other historians argue that Henry was a good king, and that he left a legacy of stability. See if you agree with their points.

1 Henry and law and order

Henry dealt with problems of law and order decisively. During his long campaigns in France there was remarkably little serious disorder in England. His reign was one of the few periods of good order among the disorderly centuries of the late Middle Ages.

2 A gifted military organiser and leader

Henry planned his military expeditions very carefully and was a superb military commander – this mattered in the Middle Ages. His victories united the nation and strengthened the monarchy. If he had not died he would have conquered France and become King of France.

3 Henry built firm foundations for the future

Henry's infant son succeeded unchallenged and despite the fact of his age and the attacks of insanity he suffered from, he lasted as king until 1461– a tribute to the firm foundations established by Henry V.

Summary task

1 Award each of the above 'for' and 'against' arguments marks out of 10.

2a) Construct a timeline for Henry's reign. Put on it the ten most important events that tell us something about how good a king he was. You will want to think about the following:

- Did he keep the barons happy?
- Did he keep law and order?
- Did he look after the ordinary people?
- Did he defend the country and have military victories?

b) Then use the timeline to draw a graph to show how well Henry was doing at different times in his reign. Do this by adding a vertical axis, labelled 1–10, and plot Henry's 'scores' above each event.

2.4 *Owain Glyndwr: a Welsh hero*

In the 1980s a secret organisation began burning Welsh holiday homes belonging to English people. The organisation was named Meibion Glyndwr (the Sons of Glendower). It was a nationalist movement violently opposed to the loss of Welsh culture, and was formed in response to the housing crisis created by English people buying second homes in Wales and putting house prices beyond the reach of locals. The name of the organisation was chosen to reflect the struggles of another Welsh patriot against the English, 600 years ago.

Who was Owain Glyndwr?

● **SOURCE 1**

Owain was one of the greatest patriots Wales has ever known.

His name has become a symbol of pride and freedom.

He sacrificed everything for a dream, of Wales as a nation, governing itself with its own institutions and universities. Where he died is not known, and the location of his grave has become one of the great mysteries of Welsh history.

It is surely fitting that the people of Wales, and Welsh communities everywhere, should mark the anniversary and the millennium by honouring his contribution to their heritage.

This passage comes from the website of the Owain Glyndwr Society which was formed in 1996. If you go to the 100 Welsh Heroes website you will find that in a vote for the greatest Welsh heroes, Owain came second with 2309 votes, narrowly losing out to Aneurin Bevan.

● **SOURCE 2**

His name inspires us to be proud of our country – no other person's name can conjure up the spirit and pride of a nation better than his.

Owain Glyndwr was the first Welsh leader to unite the people of Wales. People followed him because he inspired them.

These are some of the comments posted on www.100welshheroes.com.

● **SOURCE 3**

No name is so frequently invoked in Wales as that of Owain Glyndwr, a potent figurehead of Welsh nationalism ever since he rose up against the occupying English in the first few years of the fifteenth century.

Since 1410 most Welsh people most of the time have abandoned any idea of independence as unthinkable. But since 1410 most Welsh people, at some time or another, if only in some secret corner of the mind, have been 'out with Owain and his barefoot scrubs'. For the Welsh mind is still haunted by its lightening-flash vision of a people that was free.

A Welsh historian writing in 1985.

● SOURCE 4

A drawing of Owain
Glyndwr.

Discussion point

What impressions of Owain do you get from Sources 1–3? Choose key words that sum him up. Does the picture of Owain fit these descriptions of him? Do you notice any differences or similarities with the English kings you have studied?

Why is Owain still a hero to many Welsh people?

Wales in 1400

To understand Owain's reputation we first have to remember what had been happening to Wales. It had been gradually losing its independence since the Norman Conquest of 1066. William I had given land along the border with England (the Marches) to his barons. They had gradually seized more land in the south and east of Wales. However, the rest of Wales remained under the control of Welsh princes. That is, until Edward I's reign. He defeated the last of the Welsh princes, made his eldest son Prince of Wales, and introduced English law, officials and taxes.

However, English control of Wales was never complete and on 14 September, 1400, Owain Glyndwr was proclaimed Prince of Wales. This was to be the final bid by the Welsh to regain their lost independence. It began a revolt against English rule that would last for over ten years.

Where did Owain Glyndwr come from?

Owain was an unusual rebel – he came from a rich, landed family and owned estates in north-east Wales. He studied law in London and fought in Richard II's army in Scotland in 1385. An ordinary, respectable gentleman, you might think.

However, there was another side to him. Owain was descended from the Welsh princes of Powys on his father's side, and from the Princes of Deheubarth on his mother's side. Not only did this mean he could claim the title of Prince of Wales, it also meant that he was connected to many of the important Welsh families and that he would have support in both north and south Wales.

The rebellion

The factor that triggered the revolt seems to have been a dispute between Owain and another landowner over land. Owain could not get any justice from Henry IV or Parliament and his anger over this seems to have led him to declare himself in 1400 as Prince of Wales.

1400   Owain and his supporters attacked Ruthin and many other towns in north-east Wales. Henry IV sent an army across north Wales, looting and burning as it went. Many of the Welsh submitted. Owain fled to the hills.

1401   Owain had victories in mid-Wales and in the south. He then attacked Caernarfon Castle in the north. Hundreds flocked to support him, including members of the uchelwyr (the leading Welsh families). Henry sent another army but Owain used guerrilla tactics and simply avoided a pitched battle.

1402   Owain had further successes. Henry sent three armies into Wales but they were driven back by torrential rain, hail and snow. The English soldiers began to believe that Owain was in league with the devil and could control the weather. The English were hit by quick ambushes by the much more mobile Welsh.

1403   Henry Percy, an important English noble, rose up in rebellion against Henry. The king acted swiftly and defeated Percy at Shrewsbury before the Welsh could arrive and help him. Owain continued to capture towns and castles in north and south Wales.

1404   The years 1404–05 were the high point of the rebellion. Owain made an alliance with France. He took the castles of Harlech and Aberystwyth and controlled nearly the whole of Wales. He summoned a Parliament showing that he was setting himself up as a prince of an independent state.

1405   Owain reached an agreement with Edmund Mortimer (whose nephew had a strong claim to the throne) and Thomas Percy, Earl of Northumberland. Owain was to have control of an enlarged Wales, Mortimer the south of England and Percy the Midlands and the north. But it never came to anything.

A French force landed at Milford Haven and joined up with Owain. They marched into England as far as Worcester but then Owain turned back. He wanted to concentrate on Wales and was not interested in toppling the English king.

1406–10   The tide began to turn. The sheer power and size of the English army began to tell and whole communities submitted to Henry. In 1408 the English took Harlech Castle. Owain's family was taken prisoner. He disappeared into the hills and was never heard of again – giving strength to the idea that like King Arthur, he had not died and would return.

● **SOURCE 5**

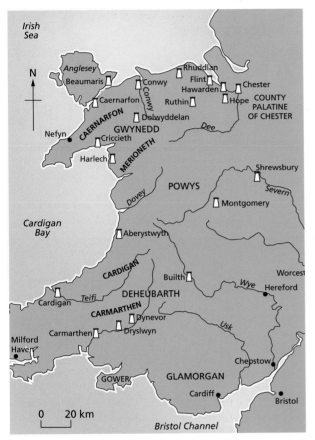

A map of Wales showing places involved in Owain's rebellion.

The rebellion was clearly not just about Owain's dispute with his neighbour. Why was nearly the whole of Wales ready to rise up? How well did Owain led the rebellion?

Prophecies

For centuries Welsh poets had made prophecies that a great prince would appear who would free Wales from English rule. Owain with his royal blood appeared to the Welsh to be the person they had been waiting for! When a comet appeared in the sky during the rebellion in 1402 the Welsh bards declared it was a sign that Wales would be free.

Henry's problems

Owain was lucky in that Henry was busy dealing with Scotland for much of the time and he could not even trust many of his own nobles in England.

Charisma

There is no doubt that Owain had the personal charisma that made people loyal to him. How else did a tiny country like Wales maintain a rebellion against England for over ten years? In all those years he was never betrayed by his own people and, as we have seen, his charisma still works today for many Welsh people.

A proper prince

Owain was determined to appear like a proper head of state. He summoned a Parliament with representatives from all over Wales and tried to act like the head of a proper government. He was joined by leading Welsh bishops, lawyers and civil servants – just the kind of people he needed to run a government. His supporters were even collecting the taxes that should have gone to the English king. It was important that he had the support of many of the Welsh ruling families.

Anti-English feelings

During the fourteenth century Wales suffered from the taxes levied by English kings fighting the Hundred Years War against France. The Black Death had also caused much disruption and hardship.

The Welsh ruling families (the uchelwyr) were also unhappy. The king was replacing them as his local officials with Englishmen. With them came their supporters and tenants. Also, in some of the towns the Welsh were not allowed to become burgesses (they were the people who ran the towns). All this led to seething anti-English feelings.

This explains why at the first signs of rebellion Welsh students and labourers working in England sped back to Wales to support Owain.

During the rebellion Henry passed more anti-Welsh laws, for example they were banned from gathering in groups and from carrying arms. This just caused more resentment.

Owain the military leader

Owain was more than a leader of a band of guerrilla fighters. He, and many of his supporters, had a lot of military experience fighting for English kings in France and Scotland. The fact that he was able to lay siege to castles suggests he had artillery.

At the same time, he handled his forces well. He often avoided pitched battles and used hit-and-run tactics. His forces were mobile: one moment they were in the north, the next they were in the south. The large, cumbersome and slow English army found this difficult to cope with.

Alliances

Owain realised that if he was to set up an independent national state he needed allies, so he made alliances with France and with the Percys and Edmund Mortimer.

Wales and weather

Owain was also helped by the mountainous nature of much of Wales and by the Welsh weather!

Discussion point

How far did Owain succeed in making himself like the other kings you have studied? Did he show the qualities needed to be a successful king?

● **SOURCE 6**

● **SOURCE 7**

The statue of Owain in
City Hall, Cardiff.

A twentieth-century painting
of Owain.

● **SOURCE 8**

A painting from *c.*1805
of Owain (standing)
plotting with Henry
Percy, Earl of
Northumberland, his
brother, the Earl of
Worcester, and Edmund
Mortimer before the
Battle of Shrewsbury.

Discussion point

What different
impressions of Owain
do the pictures in
Sources 6–8 give? Can
you think why they
give such different
impressions of the
same person?

The picture gallery

Task

On the following pages you will see how the three kings have been portrayed over the ages. What impression is each picture trying to create of the king? How does it do this? How has the way each king is portrayed over time changed?

John

● SOURCE 1

A medieval picture of John feeding dogs.

● SOURCE 2

A twentieth-century copy of an eighteenth-century engraving of John used on a cigarette card.

● SOURCE 3

The head of the effigy of John from his tomb in Worcester Cathedral. It was made about twenty years after his death.

● SOURCE 4

John in the Walt Disney film *Robin Hood*.

● SOURCE 5

A modern cartoon of John.

Edward

● **SOURCE 6**

A twentieth-century copy of an eighteenth-century engraving of Edward used on a cigarette card.

● **SOURCE 7**

A medieval drawing of Edward.

● **SOURCE 8**

John Balliol, King of Scotland, doing homage to Edward in 1292. From a medieval drawing.

● **SOURCE 9**

An eighteenth-century engraving of Edward depicted holding a sword.

● **SOURCE 10**

Edward I as portrayed in a still from the film *Braveheart*.

Henry

● **SOURCE 11**

A medieval manuscript showing Henry V and Charles VI of France agreeing the Treaty of Troyes.

● **SOURCE 12**

A portrait of Henry V painted in the late sixteenth century.

● **SOURCE 13**

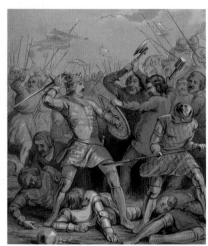

A picture of Henry from a children's annual published in 1849.

● **SOURCE 14**

A picture of Henry being presented with a book by a poet. From a book about medieval dresses and decorations published in 1858.

● **SOURCE 15**

A twentieth-century photograph of Laurence Olivier as Henry V in Shakespeare's play.

A ragbag of sources

On the next few pages is a collection of sources about the three kings and Owain Glyndwr. This is for you to dip into, especially when you are working on the externally set task. They come from different periods and give you lots of different opinions. But be careful – you need to test these opinions against what you know about the kings, as well as thinking about who wrote the source and for what purpose.

King John

● SOURCE 1

John crushed his own people and favoured foreigners. He was a lion to his own people but a lamb to foreigners and rebels. He had lost the duchy of Normandy and many other territories through laziness. Foul as it is, Hell itself is defiled by the fouler presence of King John.

Matthew Paris, a monk writing in 1235. Look back to page 67 for information about him.

● SOURCE 2

John sat as a judge. His lively mind and keen intelligence helped him deal with the cases brought before him. No king of England was ever so unlucky. From the moment when France came into the strong hands of Phillip II his conquest of Normandy was only a matter of time.

This is from a historian writing in 1951.

● SOURCE 3

The king was greatly irritated by their response. In anger and in fury he ordered his sheriffs that they should injure the monks by whatever means they could. They should persecute them and show them no justice in their law-suits.

Ralph of Diceto, dean of St Paul's Cathedral in London, in 1200 described John's reaction when he demanded money from Cistercian monks and they refused.

● SOURCE 4

When it was announced that the body of the bishop was approaching the city, the people rushed out in a crowd to the funeral procession. John, putting aside royal pomp, with the archbishops, heads bowed, humbly put the coffin on their shoulders and carried the holy burden for some time, ignoring the mud of the streets.

Writing at the time, Ralph, Abbot of Coggeshall describes John's actions at the funeral of Hugh, Bishop of Lincoln in 1201.

● SOURCE 5

The king ordered the few monks who remained at Canterbury to be expelled, and all the monks in the country to be regarded as public enemies. The whole of England was fined and taxed heavily. The people were forced to pay at first a quarter of their money, then a third, then a half. He especially imposed great afflictions on the men of the Cinque Ports. For he hanged some of them and put others to the sword. Therefore the rich and the poor left England. Theirs was a thankless pilgrimage to avoid the enormous cruelty of the king.

Gervase, a monk at Canterbury Cathedral priory at the time, describes events in 1208 during John's struggle with the Pope.

● **SOURCE 6**

King John set in motion a deed of great memory. For when the forest officials harassed many in all parts of England with new demands for money, the king seeing the misery of the people forced the officials to swear that they would only exact the amount which they collected in the days of his father.

The Barnwell chronicler, an anonymous monk at Barnwell Priory, was regarded as the most neutral of the contemporary writers, 1212.

● **SOURCE 7**

John was indeed a great prince but scarcely a happy one. He was kind to outsiders but a plunderer of his own people, trusting strangers rather than his subjects, wherefore he was deserted by his own men and, in the end, little mourned.

Also written by the Barnwell chronicler, shortly after John's death.

● **SOURCE 8**

John's brother Richard was seen as perfect; John was reviled as shifty, rapacious, cruel, vindictive and self-serving. But they had much more in common than the cartoon stereotypes allow for. John was detested for his cold-blooded execution of twenty-eight sons, taken as hostages from the Welsh princes and nobles with whom he was warring.

But Richard slaughtered 2700 hostages at the siege of Acre.

A historian writing in 2000.

King Edward I

● **SOURCE 9**

*He is a lion by his pride
 and ferocity;
but he is a leopard by his
 inconstancy and
 changeableness,
changing his word and
 his promises,
excusing himself with
 fine words.*

A poem written in the 1260s.

● **SOURCE 10**

He had in him the two wisdoms, not often found: an ability of judgement in himself, and a readiness to hear the judgement of others. He was not easily provoked into passion, but once in passion, not easily appeased, as was seen by his dealing with the Scots; towards whom he showed at first patience, and at last severity. If he be criticised for his many taxations, he may be justified by his good use of them; for never a prince laid out his money to more honour of himself, or good of his kingdom.

Sir Richard Baker writes in his *A Chronicle of the Kings of England*, published in 1643, a time of great difficulty for the English monarchy. The book was dedicated to Charles, Prince of Wales (the future Charles II).

● **SOURCE 11**

Edward I, nicknamed 'Longshanks' due to his great height and stature, was perhaps the most successful of the medieval monarchs. The first twenty years of his reign marked a high point of cooperation between crown and community. In these years, Edward made great strides in reforming government, consolidating territory, and defining foreign policy. He possessed the strength his father lacked and reasserted royal power.

Edward held to the concept of community, and although at times unscrupulously aggressive, ruled with the general welfare of his subjects in mind. He perceived the crown as judge of the proper course of action for the realm and its chief legislator; royal authority was granted by law and should be used for the public good, but that same law also granted protection to the king's subjects. A king should rule with the advice and consent of those whose rights were in question. The level of interaction between king and subject allowed Edward considerable freedom in achieving his goals.

From the Britannica website.

● SOURCE 12

Edward never got a chance to fight that last campaign. The covetous king did die, leaving a mess for his son to deal with as best he could. The mess he left behind is what strikes me most about Edward I. The power he inherited was very great, unprecedented in centuries. His personal talents were exceptional. His situation seemed to offer great opportunities for extending his rulership even further. But despite the conquest of Wales, Edward, so popular in his youth, lost the devotion of the political class long before he died. They resented his demands and feared his techniques of rule, which verged on the arbitrary. He bequeathed to his son great debts, an endless guerrilla war on the northern frontier, and a restive baronage.

From a website about Edward I.

● SOURCE 13

Edward I was a warrior of huge physical strength. Contrary to a once-fashionable notion, he was not a visionary moderniser. By the standards of his time, he was conventional, conservative, even conformist. It was not just the Scots whom he hammered. His energy was felt in all parts of the British Isles, so much so that he has been said to initiate a 'British Century'.

A historian writing in 1999.

King Henry V

● SOURCE 14

And so Henry came to Westminster, where he gave thanks again at the shrine of St Edward in the Abbey, and that night held a feast in the Hall. The rapture of the people was not for their glorious victory alone, but was a sign of how the nation's heart had gone to its King. There was no memory of any Prince, who had ruled his people in war with more personal labour, kindliness, or courage, or who had borne himself more manfully in the field. Neither was there record in the Chronicles and Annals of old that any King of England had gone forth and performed so much in so short a time, and returned again to his own with so great and so glorious a triumph.

An eye-witness account of the celebrations after Agincourt, written by a clergyman working in the king's service and who went with him to France.

● SOURCE 15

He [Henry V] was a prince of a high understanding and of a great will to keep justice. The poor folk loved him above all others. For he was careful to defend the poorer folk, and to protect them from the violence and wrong that most of the nobles had done to them.

From the memoirs of an official who worked for Charles VI, King of France.

● SOURCE 16

To his contemporaries Henry was the flower of Christian chivalry. He stands in history as the true type of the medieval hero-king. His strong sense of personal dignity and of the kingly office made him seem proud. By his subjects he was held in such fear that none dared disobey his orders. Disobedience he punished with merciless severity. But underneath lay a gentle consideration for others and in his ordinary relations he showed himself courteous and friendly to all men.

A historian writing in 1901.

● SOURCE 17

Faithlessness to old friends was part of the normal pattern of Henry's behaviour. He had turned on his beloved advisers and comrades-in-arms, Harry and Thomas Percy, at the battle of Shrewsbury in 1403. The most notorious case was that of Sir John Oldcastle, a battlefield friend, whom Henry burned to death for heresy at the start of his reign.

Henry had no right to the crown of France – after all, he had no right to that of England either. According to the legend, the war displayed Henry's military genius. Really, it was a story of gambler's luck. At first, Henry probably envisaged no more than a raid where the English would grab what they could. But a superior French army got stuck in the mud at Agincourt and Henry did what every gambler does with unexpected winnings: he increased his stake, bidding to rule France in reality. He also began, on the field of Agincourt, a career as a war criminal, massacring prisoners in defiance of the conventions. Even so, the French hated each other more than they hated him. So he was able to prolong victory. The policy was never likely to succeed: the war overstretched English resources and left the parts of France which Henry conquered prostrate with depredations and disease.

Adapted from an article entitled 'The Myth of Henry V', on the BBC history website, by the historian Felipe Fernandez-Armesto.

● SOURCE 18

With Shakespeare's gorgeous words ringing forever in our ears, it's impossible not to think of Henry V first and foremost as a warlord. But the lesson he took from the mistakes of his predecessors was that to survive and prosper, a king of England needed to be both messiah and manager. He knew when to stamp on the quarrels of the magnates and when to stroke them into consent. He possessed in spadefuls the critical psychological skill of making everyone in his immediate circle feel trusted and honoured. He made the political community confident that the king's business was also the country's.

A historian writing in 2000.

Owain Glyndwr

● SOURCE 19

Boldly flaunting on his shining helmet a scarlet flamingo feather, with his lance broken and snapped off into no more than a dagger, he drove the Scots back howling with fear like wild goats. His attack was so swift and fierce that no grass nor corn would grow in his tracks.

A description by a Welsh poet of the time of Owain fighting in Scotland in 1385.

● SOURCE 20

Of Owain's attraction for the men of his own time we have ample proof. For fifteen years, amid a divided Welsh population, only one-twelfth that of England and having an even smaller proportion of wealth and resources, he had kept the flame of rebellion alight. He must have had some remarkable personal magnetism which drew men to him and held their loyalty. That sway he has continued to exercise over the affections of Welshmen down to our own day. Though there is so much that is unknown it is impossible to resist his attraction. Perhaps it is partly because his deeds and his final fate, like those of King Arthur, are wrapped in mystery that he holds so potent an appeal for Welshmen.

The view of a Welsh historian writing in 1966.

● **SOURCE 21**

No name is so frequently invoked in Wales as that of Owain Glyndwr, a potent figurehead of Welsh nationalism ever since he rose up against the occupying English in the first few years of the fifteenth century. Little is known about the man described in Shakespeare's Henry IV, Part I *as 'not in the roll of common men'. There seems little doubt that the charismatic Owain fulfilled many of the mystical medieval prophecies about the rising up of the red dragon. He was of aristocratic stock and his blue blood furthered his claim as Prince of Wales, being directly descended from the princes of Powys and Cyfeiliog.*

From a website about Welsh castles.

● **SOURCE 22**

Folk tales in the village say that a horse was kept saddled day and night in case Owain needed to get away quickly. Many historians believe he returned to his hills to die.

  His grave is beside no church, neither under the shadow of any ancient yew. It is in a spot safer and more sacred still. Rain does not fall on it, hail nor sleet chill it. It is forever green with the green of eternal spring. Bathed in sunlight; close and warm and dear it lies, sheltered from all storms, from all cold or grey oblivion. Time shall not touch it; decay shall not dishonour it; for that grave is in the heart of every true Cymro. There, for ever, from generation unto generation, grey Owain's heart lies dreaming on, dreaming on, safe for ever and for ever.

Written by a Welshman in 1905.

● **SOURCE 23**

He was more than a revolutionary; he campaigned internationally for an independent Welsh Nation, church and state, at a time when attaining it would have been practically unthinkable.

  Owain Glyndwr was the first Welsh leader to unite the PEOPLE of Wales. People followed him not due to some Middle Ages feudalism but because he inspired them.

Comments from people on a website about Welsh heroes.

● **SOURCE 24**

Shakespeare's portrayal, perhaps the most influential in shaping Glyndwr's image among an English public, presented him not only as a fierce warrior endowed with supernatural powers, but also as a cultured and dignified figure 'not in the roll of common men'. For nineteenth-century supporters of Welsh liberal ideals Glyndwr was identified as the prime inspiration of their own cherished aims – a Welsh parliament, a reformed and liberated church, and a national university.

From the *Oxford Dictionary of National Biography.*

Summing up

This chart has been designed to help you organise your thoughts when you need to compare the four monarchs/leaders you have been studying. On your own copy, in each section, write down as many examples as you can of achievements and failures for each king in each of the five areas listed on the left. Just write a title down for each example e.g. Agincourt. Then award each monarch a mark out of 10 for each category. Take into account their successes and failures. By adding the score up you will end up with a mark out of 50 for each monarch. Compare your scores with other people in your class. Discuss why you have different scores from them.

The timelines and graphs that you drew for each of the monarchs will help you with this exercise.

	John	Edward	Henry	Owain	Total score
Law and order					
Looking after ordinary people					
Keeping the barons happy					
Defending the country and having military victories					
Leaving a strong legacy for the next king					

The externally set task

How to succeed with the task

At the end of your course of study of medieval kings you will have to complete what the exam board calls an externally set task. You will be given a question and you will have four hours to research, plan and write an answer. These four hours will probably be spread across several of your normal history lessons.

Below is an example of the type of question you will be given.

'The most important quality that a medieval king needed was the ability to be a successful leader on the battlefield.'

How far do the sources you have researched convince you that this statement is correct?

Before you start

From the very start, there are four important things to remember:

1 There is no right answer. What will impress the examiners is how well you support your arguments.
2 The examiner is interested in how well you have answered the question, not in how much you have found out or how much you can write.
3 The question says 'how far do the sources you have researched convince you that this statement is correct?'. This means you need to comment on the sources you have used – have they been useful, do you trust them, do they differ from each other, are there things they do not tell you about? Make sure you have used a wide range of different types of sources: from the medieval period and from later; written sources and illustrations.
4 You must manage your time properly. There is no point in having lots of notes if you don't have time to write your final answer. It would seem sensible to spend roughly two hours on your research, half an hour on sorting everything out and an hour and a half writing up your findings. But this is just a rough guide. A lot depends on how quickly you work and how easy you find the question. But don't worry: a short, well-argued answer that keeps to the question will score more highly than a long, rambling one that contains lots of material but doesn't get to the point.

How to tackle the task

1 Think about what you know already

- What other qualities did a medieval king need? Draw up a checklist.
- Think about how important it was to be a good military leader. Why did this matter? How does it compare with other qualities medieval kings needed? Was it more, or less, important? Or did this vary from reign to reign because of different circumstances?

2 Planning

- It is always useful to think about how you might organise your answer before you do your research. This will help you to keep your notes in an order that will be easy to use later. Of course, you might need to alter your plan a bit once you have done the research.
- For this particular question it will be better to use the different qualities kings needed as the basic sections, rather than write about each king separately.
- However, you will need first to have a brief introduction explaining what qualities kings needed and why they needed them.
- You also need to remember that you will need, at some stage, to compare the importance of these qualities.

Your plan might look something like this:

Introduction   Briefly discuss what qualities kings needed, and why they needed them. A statement by you that you are going to compare the importance of military leadership with other qualities.

A section on military leadership   Use actual examples for this. Discuss how important it was for a medieval king to be a good military leader using real examples from the three reigns. Explain examples of where a king was made stronger, or weaker, by the strength or failure of his military leadership. Was it more important for some kings? Why? Reach and support a judgement about the importance of military leadership.

   Remember: do not use every example you find; select the best and explain and analyse them carefully. And keep to the question!

   Remember to comment on the sources you have been using.

Two or three sections on other important qualities   In each of these sections you should not write about a quality by itself – you need to discuss how it compared in terms of importance with military leadership. Can you find examples of when military leadership was most important? Can you find examples of when another quality was more important? How far did a king's success in another area compensate for his weaknesses in military leadership?

   Remember: do not use every example you find; select the best and explain and analyse them carefully. And keep to the question!

   Remember to comment on the sources you have been using.

Conclusion   This is where you sum up the main points you have made and directly answer the question. Make sure that you do not introduce new material here. Everything you write should be based on earlier parts of your work. Remember that you do not have to end with a definite yes or no to the question. You might decide that military leadership was generally most important but there was the odd occasion when this was not the case.

One important thing to remember:

As you do your research you will find that there are different opinions about how good or bad these kings were. These views might come from people at the time, or they may come from later. You need to include in your work an explanation of some of these different opinions and reasons why you agree with some and not others. You might also want to explain why these different opinions exist. However, all this must be used as part of answering the question; it must not be tacked on the end.

To sum up:

Introduction	– a brief discussion of the qualities kings needed
Section 1	– explain why military leadership was an important quality
	– give specific examples from the kings you have studied
Sections 2 & 3	– explain why other qualities (perhaps 2 or 3) were needed as well
	– give specific examples from the kings you have studied
	– compare the importance of military leadership with the importance of the other qualities
	– explain whether some qualities were more important than others at certain times or in certain circumstances
Conclusion	– clearly state your final answer to the question with some clinching reasons.

3 Starting your research

- The task asks you to research sources. You will need to use evidence from a wide range of sources to back up what you are going to say. You should be looking for evidence of what the kings actually did, what people at the time said about them and what has been said about them since. Don't forget illustrations – these can show us different views as well.
- Remember to think about the reliability and usefulness of the sources you use.
- Start with the information you have in this book and with other notes you may already have made to see what examples you can find of the success or failure of the three medieval kings as military leaders. And don't forget to dip into the ragbag.
- Remember to think about how important their successes and failures in military leadership were for these kings.
- Use your notes and other information you have already to see what examples you can find of the three kings demonstrating, or failing to demonstrate, other important qualities.

4 Widening your research

- You will also need to go beyond your own notes and books. This might involve you using the internet and libraries. Some useful internet addresses are given below. But before you rush away and print off hundreds of pages from a website, stand back and think: what am I looking for? Go back to your plan and look for evidence that fits into it and helps answer the question. **Be selective**. A couple of good examples that are well explained and help you answer the question are much more use than dozens of pages of information much of which is not relevant.

  http://en.wikipedia.org   www.bartelby.com
  www.bbc.co.uk/history   www.royal.gov.uk
  www.britannica.com/
  www.spartacus.schoolnet.co.uk
  www.historylearningsite.co.uk
  www.schoolhistory.co.uk
  www.aginc.net/battle
  www.geocities.com/beckster05/Agincourt/AgBattle.html
  www.owain-glyndwr-soc.org.uk

- This wider research will help you to add to what you already know from your own notes and books.
- Remember to look for different opinions. Are these different opinions supported by the evidence you have found about the kings?
- Make sure you keep organised. Keep your notes organised so that they fit into your plan. Keep the notes for each section separate, on different pages.
- Keep a note of all the sources you use – you will need to list them all at the end of your answer.

5 Write up your findings

- At this stage there is always the danger of being overwhelmed by all the things you have found out and all the notes you have made. It is important to remember that the examiner will not be interested simply in how much you have found out. What they most want to know is **how well have you answered the question?**
- Be ruthless – throw out all the information you have collected that looked interesting but does not help you to answer the question. If you have dozens of examples that are useful you will have to decide which are best – you will not be able to use all of them.
- Take another look at your plan: is it working? Does it help you to directly answer the question? If it doesn't, you may have to change it a bit.
- Back up what you say by referring to the sources you have researched and by giving examples from the reigns of the kings.
- Remember to explain that there are different opinions about some of the things you are writing about – explain why you think people have different views and why you think some are better than others.
- Do your best to communicate your findings clearly, and use correct grammar and spelling.

Good luck!

Index